"Mr. D."
Una bella vita

TO: Kaley
From: Mr D.

Dedications

To my parents
While I was growing up, I loved you
Now that you are gone, I miss you

To my brothers and sisters
We were close growing up
And we are closer getting older

To my wife
Who stood next to me
And shared our success and my love

To all my children
It was fun watching you grow
Now it's a pleasure to work with you

To my grandchildren
You are my life
Your Nonno's only wish is to sing and dance
at each of your weddings

And to all my dear family
Never forget where you came from

Vincenzo DiCosimo

"Mr. D." Una bella vita

as told to
Mike Tenszen

SOLEIL

Layout and Design: Anthony Mollica, José Cortés
Cover photograph: Precious LaPlante, Port Colborne

éditions SOLEIL *publishing inc.*

Canada: P.O. Box 847 • Welland, Ontario L3B 5Y5 • Tel. / Fax: (905) 788-2674
USA: P.O. Box 890 • Lewiston, NY 14092-0890 • Tel. / Fax: (905) 788-2674
Fax Order Desk: 1-800-261-0833
soleil@soleilpublishing.com   www.soleilpublishing.com

ISBN   1-894935-31-4   Printed in Canada

Library and Archives Canada Cataloguing in Publication

DiCosimo, Vincenzo, 1936-

Mr. D. : Una bella vita / Vincenzo DiCosimo; with Mike Tenszen.

ISBN 978-1-894935-31-4

1. DiCosimo, Vincenzo, 1936-.   2. Hotelkeepers—Canada—Biography.   3. Italian Canadians—Biography.   4. Immigrants—Canada—Biography.

I. Tenszen, Mike, 1944- II. Title.

TX910.5.D43A3 2007   647.94092   C2007-905289-4

Table of Contents

Table of Contents

A Message From "Mr. D."

Some people have asked me why I wanted this biography written. That's easy. It's not to brag about myself. I'm no better than anybody else. I'm just lucky. I always tried to do my best; do what I had to do. I worked as hard as I could; I tried to look after my wonderful family. And they've been with me all the way.

I love them all. They are my life. This book is dedicated to them.

The book subtitle is Una bella vita. And, it *has* been a good life.

You want to know something? You can make money and you can lose it. It's just money. Money doesn't mean anything. Honestly, I really mean it. The only thing I hope I have "earned" in my life is the love and respect of my family and my friends.

By the way, I urge everyone to tell his or her own family story. They should just let it out. They should get somebody to write it down. If you put it down on paper, people are free to pick up the book. That's the advantage of writing your own book. I always say this: Everybody's got a little story. *You* have a story to tell and I encourage you to do it. For your own family. If you read this book by any chance, or hear about this book, think about doing the exact same thing.

What stops some people from doing it is that it takes a lot of guts to make the decision to proceed. Some people think they would like to tell their story, but they don't feel it would be interesting. You'd be surprised how interesting your life is. I think everybody's life is interesting.

I tell my kids and grandkids about my own parents and grandparents. I tell them stories about my father's side and my mother's side. There are some interesting stories. I was telling my little grandson, Vincent, the other night – he's the youngest grandchild – I said: "Listen, Vincie, before you know where you are going you've got to know where you come from." And his father said "Nonno is right, you got to know your roots."

When Ida and I came over from Italy we had no money and couldn't speak a word of English – but we had hope in our hearts.

Maybe that was the experience of your own relatives. Get writing!

Now I would like to say something else to you from my heart. I love my birthplace, Italy. My family and I go there as often as we can to see family and friends. But, back in 1955, when I was 19, I chose a new life in Canada. I made the right decision. Canada has been good to me. I am a very proud Canadian. Canada gave me whatever I wanted, some big opportunities – as it gave to other immigrants from all the countries of the world.

I don't gamble much, even though there's a big casino right across the street from our hotel. Okay, maybe I put out a couple of bucks on the golf course. What I am really saying is that Ida and I took our biggest gamble on Canada nearly a half-century ago. Omigod, we hit the jackpot!

I hope you will enjoy my little story.

Newly arrived in Niagara Falls, the 20-year-old Vince DiCosimo, working as a low-paid labourer, had this photo taken at a Niagara Falls studio in 1956.

Introduction

by Mike Tenszen

So who is "Mr. D."?

Well, at times he was a ditch digger, fruit vendor, battery factory worker, welder, car wash proprietor, steel fabrication company owner, snack bar operator.

A half-century ago he spoke no English and had no money. Now he can and he does.

For a Grade 5 dropout, "Mr. D.", Niagara Falls entrepreneur Vincenzo DiCosimo, 71, has done quite well. He is, just now, in charge of a $200-million project to build a 58-storey addition to his spectacular Hilton Niagara Falls Fallsview, which his family company opened in 2000. The new luxury Hilton Fallsview, with more than 1,000 suites and rooms, will soon be the tallest and largest hotel in Canada.

Vince, a feisty farm kid who was born and raised in San Lorenzo Maggiore, Benevento, Italy, now mingles with doctors, financiers, architects, lawyers, college presidents, top bankers, key politicians, and corporate leaders from all over the world. But he has never forgotten his middle-class roots in Italy nor the friends and family who were always there working beside him, backing him.

Hotel staff members call him "Mr. D." That's easiest for them. Vince's smile and laugh and happy outlook on life make him much more than a boss. If Vince is not teeing off with a bank president, he might be golfing with some of his employees. If he's not in a boardroom discussing business with bankers, he's walking around in the Hilton Niagara Falls Fallsview discussing the day's activities with staff.

Vincenzo DiCosimo

An immigrant from Italy in 1955, Vince is one of more than two million Italians who have sought new opportunities in Canada. One of the immigrants who, with their families, their hard work, and their risk taking, have built a future for themselves and their families.

Vince DiCosimo and his family are among the several most successful Niagara Falls families of Italian immigrant background who have done the most to build the famous city.

Vince says that the love and help of his wife, Ida, his hometown sweetheart, and his children, Joe, Frank, Anita and Vincent, have made it possible for him to succeed and to now be enjoying "Una bella vita," a good life.

When Vince and Ida started out in Niagara Falls in 1958, "it wasn't easy," he says. "But, at the same time, we had nothing to lose. I had myself to offer, that was it. I didn't come to Canada to work for somebody else. I was looking for an opening. I came from the bottom up."

In 1955, Vince first came to Niagara Falls from his birthplace, San Lorenzo Maggiore, Italy. He returned home to marry his hometown sweetheart, Ida Garofano, in 1958. The young couple then came back to settle in Niagara Falls, at first living with his older brother Stanley and his wife, Nicoletta.

Today, the centrepiece of the DiCosimo business holdings is the lavish, 520-room (soon to be 1,000-room) Hilton Niagara Falls Fallsview. When completed, in 2009, the new Hilton Niagara Falls Fallsview will be the highest structure in "The Roar City".

How did the farm boy from San Lorenzo rise to be one of the leading businessmen and humanitarians in the Niagara area?

In two words: hard work.

A visiting relative from Italy, dining with Vince in the Hilton, 33 storeys above the swirling mists of Niagara Falls, turned to him and asked: "You don't really own all of this, do you?"

He does.

But, why this book about this humble man?

Vince explains that he simply wishes to trace out his life on paper so that it will be part of the family record. Then, future DiCosimo generations can see how he and Ida and the children started it all.

"I wanted my life written down for my grandchildren," said Vince. "I hope other people will read it. At the end of the day, everybody has got a little story to tell. This is mine."

It didn't take long for this biographer to discover that Vince was, and is, an absolutely fearless guy who can't seem to say 'no' to any business challenge or opportunity. He is full of ideas. He loves keeping busy and fixing things himself. He won't retire.

By 1954, Vince's brother, Stanley, had left Italy and was working in Niagara Falls. The brothers eventually reunited and then embarked on a variety of manual labour jobs in Niagara Falls – the only occupations open at that time to Italian immigrants with no trades, no English.

That was then.

Flash forward now to a glittering, black tie event on Saturday night, November 5, 2005 on the Lundy's Lane tourist strip in Niagara Falls. There, at the glitzy Americana Hotel, amid a throng of hundreds of accomplished men and women in the Canadian Italian Business and Professional Association of Niagara (CIBPA), sat Vince DiCosimo, his brother Stanley, and their families. The brothers were enjoying a night of friendship with their families and business associates.

Vince DiCosimo was being honoured that night by the association for "business excellence and humanitarianism."

This book, as you shall soon see, was just a finger squeeze from not being written at all. In 1943, a German soldier could have pulled the trigger to end the life of our spunky little farm kid. Little Vincenzo – as fearless back then as he is now – was defending his grandfather, with his bare hands, by going for the throat of a marauding enemy.

It's a great war story. One of many Vince tells here.

As I learned through our many hours of interviews, Vince is a relaxed, interesting conversationalist – and also a good listener. His book was really written by him because he has great recall of the past and is refreshingly candid.

Tanya Hvilivitzky, of Niagara Falls, introduced me to "Mr. D.", and helped get the book rolling. Thanks Tanya. Her

Gianni Russo (left) who played Carlo Rizzi in *The Godfather* movie, and U.S. heavyweight boxer, "Baby Joe" Mesi, of Buffalo, were guest speakers on Nov. 5, 2005, when Vince received the "Business Excellence and Humanitarian Award" from the Canadian Italian Business and Professional Association (CIBPA) at the Americana Conference Resort and Spa in Niagara Falls.

father, Joe Hvilivitzky, a long-distance runner from Chippawa, read the manuscript, corrected errors, and made great suggestions. Thanks Joe.

Vince, Ida, and their family have been co-operative, welcoming, and far too patient with this author during the many interviews, persistent phone calls, e-mails, and constant requests for information and photos.

Professor Anthony Mollica, that hard-driving and meticulous Soleil publisher, took charge to craft this book with the same passion and expertise that made Tony such a distinguished educator, international academic, and decorated son of Italy.

I thank you all, and I hope this little story somehow properly portrays "Mr. D.", a good man, who deserves his fine family, his countless friends, his success, and a happy and healthy future.

Port Colborne, Ontario
August, 2007

1

A Surprise Florida Cruise

"Happy Birthday, Nonno!"

Vince had no idea.

"I was shocked," he said. "After the party, at night, I couldn't sleep. It was like a dream. I saw people there I never expected! It was a time to remember!"

March 13, 2006. About 100 people, family and friends, boarded a pristine white, luxury cruise ship at Palm Beach Port. They were there to lavish Vince with love, praise, and to help celebrate the 70 years since his birth in San Lorenzo Maggiore, in the province of Benevento, on March 13, 1936.

"What an amazing family you have created!" one young grandchild told her Nonno at the party. Kids say it best.

And, in the warmth of that gentle tropical evening, sun setting, moon rising, breeze wafting across all decks, there was a celebration, an exaltation really, of a good man, with a fine family, with loyal friends, good health, success, and with the deep respect earned from hard work, guts, and generosity.

Here was a man of humble beginnings, a ditch digger who climbed out, and who had reached the Bible's "three score and ten" years.

Four months in the planning, the surprise occasion was held on the 142-foot "Kathleen Windridge." The invitations, a classy card with scenes of a ship at sea, were marked: "Top Secret, Shhhhhhh!"

Vince's four children and grandchildren were there and friends flew down from Canada and relatives crossed the ocean from Italy. Grandchild Melina was in Tennessee at a rowing event, but she sent a recorded message. His children and grandchildren also voiced recorded greetings that were played at the party and recorded on a "Birthday DVD" that is already a family treasure.

Vince's brother, Vittorio, and his wife, Maria, came from San Lorenzo; his sister Dora, and husband, Giuseppe ("Peppino") came from Milano.

"They were so nervous they didn't think it was going to work," Vince said with a laugh about the secrecy and the complicated preparations for his wonderful day. His relatives from Italy had arrived three days before the March 13 party so they had to be hidden from Vince as he made his usual rounds of daily visits in Florida. For example, when his "hidden" relatives wanted to go shopping locally, they had to be kept away from The Home Depot, and Costco, two of Vince's daily haunts.

All of the party people hid aboard the cruise boat that was docked about 10 minutes away from the DiCosimo home. Vince was driven to the boat and he said that when he looked at the vessel he noticed many people on the boat – but he didn't recognize anybody.

"I saw people through the window but I just thought it was a regular dinner cruise," said the birthday boy.

His brother and sister were hidden on an upper deck of the boat and Ida was quickly warned by son Frank (just after Vince and Ida got the initial shock) that they would be coming down from the upper deck to surprise Vince. (A nurse friend was on standby in case the excitement got too much. It did, but the nurse wasn't needed.)

When his two siblings walked in on Vince: "Omigod. I'll tell you I just couldn't believe it. I don't even know how to explain it."

There were tears, hugs, laughter.

Because his sister, Dora, was recovering from breast cancer, and often told her brother she was too weak to travel, Vince said he honestly did not expect to see her at this birthday party.

"My friends were crying," said Vince. "One guy from Toronto said: 'Vince, I never, never cried in my life but I got so damned emotional that night. The way your kids organized it'." Indeed the evening was perfect due to the painstaking planning by the whole DiCosimo family, and the incredible ability of 100 people to keep a secret.

Said Vince, tears welling in his eyes recalling that exciting evening: "Even my little grandson, he's six years old, and he speaks on a recording: 'Hey, Nonno, how are you'? It was so beautiful."

Anita said that the planning for the party began back in November 2005. She admits that the "logistics" were quite involved but everybody helped out. "We all did it. But I guess I was the social convenor." Even Ida DiCosimo had no idea about the 100-guest surprise for her husband. Vince thought a few family members and friends were going to enjoy a quiet dinner aboard the cruise ship. But when he walked onto the boat both he and Ida were surprised beyond belief and then swept away in the love and good times.

Said "social convener" Anita: "We decided it was between the Breakers Hotel, a dinner party, or have it on the boat and we thought that people would have more fun on a dinner cruise. A lot of people were down there in Florida already and everyone else paid their own trip down. We pretended (to her father) that just a few of us were going out to dinner on a cruise. My dad said 'let's go for it'."

She said that she and her husband, Giancarlo, and two daughters, flew down to Florida six days before the party. Anita's big job was to keep everyone out of sight of her father. "We had to keep him occupied."

Party time was a gentle, warm, moonlit night. The ship cruised the inland Florida waters for four hours while the celebrants wined and dined and hugged and danced and sang. Vince's favourite singer, Joe Monti, sang some classic Italian songs.

Anita said her father was "absolutely shocked" with the surprise event. "We talked about it for a long time."

Shortly after the party, Dora, Vittorio and Stanley got together and wrote up their thoughts about their brother:

"Our brother is intelligent, so easy to converse with and able to have so many fine, reciprocal, friendly relationships. He is sincere and makes friends easily. Vince is so sensitive toward needy people. He is generous with everyone.

"Vincenzo is genuine, honest, affectionate, lovable and courteous.

"He has high morals. He expects good behaviour. He always sets an example (for his family) by respecting the law and observing the traditions of the place in which he lives. He avoids undersirable friendships.

"Our dear Vincent is always focused on achieving the best results with the minimum of energy. He is bold in his economic affairs but he is also a rational man. His ambition makes him always seek new goals.

"To our brother, his family is considered the most precious gift of his life. We know that he would sacrifice his own life for the welfare of his family."

In his recorded message to his father, played at the party, Joe DiCosimo told his father: "Boy, it just seems like yesterday that we were on a boat in Buffalo celebrating my 30th birthday. How the time flies. We spent a lot of time together over the years, and as more and more time goes by, I realize, more and more, what a special person you are. You have this natural ability to just make people feel good when they are around you. You have made us all better people. You have been a great father to me, and great grandfather to my children. If I can be half the father to my kids as you were to me, I know they will be okay. Happy Birthday Pa. I love you. Your son, Joe."

In her message to her father-in-law, Nicole, Joe's wife, said: "Hi, Pa. When I speak of you, and all the times we have shared, and the things we have done together in the 25 years I have known you, I am the envy of all. Because no one has a father-in-law, and a family as great as mine! Thanks for all you do, happy 70th birthday, lots of love, Nicole."

In his message to his father, Vincent Jr., said: "Hey, Pa, it's Vince. I just wanted to wish you a happy 70th birthday. I love you very much and I can't wait to be down in Florida with you. I hope this is a great surprise. We have been planning it for a long time. You're the best. Wish you happy birthday. I love you a lot. I love you too, ma. I didn't forget about you."

Vincent's wife, Joy, said: "Hi, Pa. It's Joy. Just wishing you a happy 70th birthday. I love you very much and I am very proud to spend this day with you."

Son Frank's wife, Barbara, said: "Pa, this is Barbara. I want to wish you a very happy 70th birthday. You are a very special person. You have always been like a father to me and I'd like to thank you for all you have done over the years. You are an amazing man and I love you very much."

Frank said: "Pa, it's your son, Frankie. I just want to wish you a very, very happy birthday. I'm glad that we had a chance to get all your friends and relatives there, including Dora and Vittorio. Hopefully you are having a great time and I love you very very much. Ma, I am also thinking of you. I know this is a special night for pa, but I know you, ma, are a big part of this family."

Anita said: "Hi, Pa. I hope you are having great time tonight with all your family and friends around you. I just want to let you know that you are the best father a daughter could even ask for. Thank you for always caring for me, Giancarlo, and my girls. You are simply the best. I hope you enjoy tonight and many more parties to come. I must say this one was the most challenging. But we did it! Happy 70th birthday. Love, your Anita. Hey, Ma, don't worry. We are already starting to plan your 70th party."

Giancarlo, Anita's husband, said: "Hi, Pa. 1986 was a special year for me because, not only did you become my father-in-law, but you also became one of my best friends. I thank you for that and I wish you a happy birthday. Your son-in-law, Giancarlo."

Joe Filippelli, Giancarlo's brother: "On behalf of me and my family, the first thing I want to say is thank you very much for allowing my family into your family. And I wish you lots of luck. I hope God keeps you healthy as long as He can because we love you very much. Happy Birthday."

Joe DiCosimo, Vince's brother Stan's son: "Hi, Uncle Vince. Happy birthday on your 70th birthday. All the best. Happiest wishes for you. Sorry I won't be able to be there with you but I'll be waiting for you here back home and we will have a drink together. Zia Ida, I love you too."

"Hi, Uncle Vince, this is Anna (Stan's daughter). Happy Birthday from me, Gabriele (Rossi) and Vanessa. We're so glad to be here on this special occasion with you. Have a nice 70th birthday. You are a very special uncle. And that will always be. P.S. We always have a great laugh, you and me. Happy birthday. Again, God bless you and we'll always be together. We love you."

"Happy birthday, Nonno, it's Alexandria (grandchild). I hope you have a great 70th birthday party. I love you very much. Bye."

"Happy birthday, Nonno," said Alissa (grandchild). "I know you have had a great 70 years because you have spent it with love and care. We have had so many good memories together and I can't wait for more to come. Lots of love and best wishes, Alissa."

"Hey, Nonno, it's Lauren (grandchild). I just wanted to say happy 70th birthday. Have a wonderful day. Can you believe 70 years have gone by? But when you have a great life, time just seems to fly. Thank you for everything and all that you do, because we wouldn't be here if it weren't for you. So, enjoy the night spent on this beautiful yacht with family and friends who sure mean a lot. So, let's all share some laughs and a smile, and let's make your 70th birthday worthwhile. Keep smiling and enjoy the party. You deserve it. I love you so much. Happy birthday. Love Lauren."

Linnea (grandchild): "On a yacht in Palm Beach celebrating your 70th birthday with all your family and friends! It doesn't get much better than this. I hope you have an amazing night. Remember it forever. I love you and happy birthday."

Marisa (grandchild): "Nonno, there are no words to begin to describe what an amazing person you are and how important you are to me. Being the first grandchild, and having you and Nonna raise me, you have become like a father to me. Experiencing Italy with just you and Nonna when I was three was just the beginning. You made sure to always be by my side, comforting me when I was scared and sad. As I continue to grow you are my protector, my teacher, and my hero. You have taught me about life and that we must take chances in order to succeed. That I must always be positive and treat people the way that I want to be treated. In you I see a man who loves and is proud of his family, a man who would go any distance to protect the ones he loves. You live with honour and pride for the person you have become and the accomplishments you have made in life. I look up to you and respect you for that. I only wish I am as lucky as Nonna. Nonno, you have made me feel like a princess. You took my hand as a little girl and guided me to the person I am today. I only hope you will never let go of my hand so that you may carry me through life, Nonno. Love Marisa. P.S. Nonno, Nick (boyfriend) wants to wish you a very happy birthday and he cannot wait to come to Ballenisles."

"Hi, Nonno, it's Melina (grandchild). Sorry I can't be there with you today I am away with my team training in Tennessee. I hope you enjoy your day, you deserve every single minute of it. So, happy birthday and I'll see you when I get home. I love you. Nonno, Steve (boyfriend) also sends his birthday wishes."

Samantha (grandchild): "Hey Nonno, I am sure you are really taken aback by all the surprises you found tonight but you deserve everything. You've got the beach, the boat, cake and presents but, most importantly, you have family and friends sitting around you that love you more than words can say. Nonno, I look at you and see a man so full of love and accomplishments. Every move you make I watch attentively and every word you say I listen so very carefully. When I was a little girl sitting so small in my pigtails you made me feel bigger than the world. I was spoiled and treated like any other child with their grandfather."

"Hi Nonno, it's Gabriella (grandchild). I am just wishing you a happy birthday. I love you. Bye."

"Hi Nonno, it's Frankie (grandchild). Congratulations on your 70th birthday. I hope you enjoy this very special evening with all of us as much as we are going to enjoy it with you. You're the best. I love you very much."

Lindsay (grandchild) said: "Dear Nonno. I will start off by saying happy 70th birthday. Over the past 16 years of my life, I have come to know you to be a compassionate, good-hearted and loving person. You never put anyone before yourself, making sure that everyone else is safe and taken care of first. You are wise beyond your words. Your stories of when you were younger captivate my mind and spark my imagination for what can be accomplished. Determination, and the mind-set that hard work pays off, is what you have instilled in our family. What an amazing family you have created. Be proud of what you have accomplished. I certainly am and there are no words given to us to express how much that truly means. Even when you are sitting in your livingroom, and no one is saying a word, I can feel that I am loved and cared for by you. Thank you for all that you have done, all that you have given us, and all that you have given to our families. I love you and, happy 70th birthday, love Lindsay."

"Hi Nonno, it's Vincent (grandchild). Happy birthday. I love you very much. I can't wait to be down there. Bye."

Vince said he was deeply moved by these tributes from his grandchildren and other relatives. One friend of his, who cried while the grandkids talked about their Nonno, said to Vince: "That's your wealth, Vince! That's your wealth!"

A year after his 70th birthday party, Vince sat down at his Niagara Falls home and talked about his grandchildren. He began by saying that when his and Ida's first grandchild, Marisa Filippelli, was born it was almost like the birth of their first child they were so happy.

At the time, Vince, who was 51, joked with a friend by saying: "I am an old father, but a young grandfather."

"At the end of the day, that is how you look at what is important in your life, your grandkids," said Vince. "We are fortunate that they are all nice kids, good kids. So far, they have never given us, or their parents, an ounce of problems. They like us and they respect us. They are close to us and we are close to them. They mean everything to me and to my wife.

"When people tell me I am wealthy, I tell them I am only wealthy because I have my family," said Vince. Money, property, and all of "that stuff, I can lose tomorrow," he adds. Money? You can "remake it." Family you cannot replace.

As a rule Vince said that he and Ida try not to tell their own children how to raise their children. On occasion, one of their four children will ask their parents about one child or another:

"Mom, dad, tell me, was I like this?"

Vince laughs when he relates what he always tells his own children.

"Nope, you were PERFECT!"

Vince said he only has a bit of advice for all his grandchildren: "One thing I advise you, make sure you have an education. That's the first thing you must do. Once you have your education then you can do whatever you want. I tell my kids, force your kids to go to school."

With four children and 11 grandchild it's tough to remember 15 birth dates, and four wedding anniversaries, Vince admits. But to the rescue comes daughter, Anita, who gives her mom and dad prior notification of these special days.

To Vince and Ida DiCosimo, their four children and their 11 grandchildren, and their in-laws, are the joys of their lives.The DiCosimo family is incredibly close, say all of its members. In touch with family by phone or personal visits daily, both Ida and Vince also keep in frequent touch with their relatives in Italy – and visit there as much as they can.

Their children and grandchildren were all born at the Greater Niagara General Hospital (GNGH) in Niagara Falls. (The DiCosimo family has made generous donations to the hospital.)

The four children, their spouses, marriage dates, their own children and birth dates, are listed here:

Joseph DiCosimo (born June 4, 1961) was married to Nicole Hessell (b. Feb. 13, 1964, GNGH) at St. Patrick's Church, Niagara Falls, on Oct. 8, 1988. Their children are Lindsay Jessica, (b. June 28, 1989); Lauren Ashley, (b. Jan. 20, 1991); Alissa Kailyn, (b. March 31, 1994.)

"Mr. D." Una bella vita

The DiCosimo family taken in 2003 at Vince and Ida's home on Cardinal Drive in Niagara Falls. *First row, from left*, are Lindsay Jessica DiCosimo, Alexandria Noelle DiCosimo, Alissa Kailyn DiCosimo, Gabriella Rose DiCosimo, and Linnea DiCosimo. *Second row, from left*, are Lauren Ashley DiCosimo, Samantha Filippelli, Ida DiCosimo, Vincent DiCosimo, Frankie DiCosimo, and Marissa Filippelli. *Third row, from left*, are Melina DiCosimo, Frank DiCosimo, Barbara DiCosimo, Joe DiCosimo, Nicole DiCosimo, Vince DiCosimo, Giancarlo Filippelli, Anita Filippelli, Vince DiCosimo Jr., and Joy DiCosimo. (Photo by Carlos Marquez)

Frank DiCosimo (born July 24, 1962) was married to Barbara Ellison, (b. Jan. 23, 1962 in England) at St. Patrick's Church, Oct. 5, 1985. Their children are Melina, (b. Dec. 8, 1987); Linnea, (b. Nov. 18, 1991); Frankie, (b. July 21, 1994.)

Anita DiCosimo (born Jan. 11, 1965) was married to Giancarlo Filippelli (b. March 2, 1961 in Italy) at St. Patrick's Church on Sept. 13, 1986. Their children are Marisa, (b. July 29, 1987), and Samantha, (b. March 9, 1991.)

Vincent DiCosimo (born July 31, 1969) was married to Joy Hessell (b. Dec. 13, 1970) at St. Patrick's Church on Sept. 10, 1994. Their children are Alexandria Noelle, (b. Nov. 3, 1995); Gabriella Rose, (b. Dec. 22, 1997); and Vincent Anthony, (b. July 31, 1999.)

These days, Vince and Ida enjoy watching their family succeed, take chances, grow, and love. Vince, who is on an active schedule of turning up for the sports activities and special occasions of his grand kids, said he would prefer to see the family stick together and all live in The Falls. But neither he nor Ida would ever hold anybody back, force them to stay in the family business, said Vince. The example of the true grit, and the drive of Vince DiCosimo inspires all of the family members. They know what he, Ida, and the kids, have accomplished through all the years.

So they all know what can be done.

2

Friends Talk About Vince

"His family is the main part of his life."

People like and admire Vince DiCosimo. Friends who speak highly of him come from every walk of life – a close business associate, a college president, a financial executive, a lawyer and former senior municipal official, a bartender, a furniture store owner, one of Canada's most innovative wine makers, a top, U.S.-based Hilton Hotels executive, and a leading Canadian corporate executive.

These people describe a family man who speaks plainly, is generous, enjoys people and parties, good food and wine, laughs a lot, and has a big heart.

Don Wilson, a Niagara real estate broker, has worked with Vince for more than 20 years on various commercial real estate transactions. "Vince is a pleasure to deal with," said Wilson. "From beginning to end he is definitely a risk taker; he is prepared to acquire (property) based on his own intuition about how he thinks he can change things around. He is not one of these fellows who must understand each and every penny. He believes in his ability and his family's to take an asset and make it something."

According to Wilson, "Mr. D." is a "big picture" type of businessman who does "not get bogged down in the colour of the building. He has been the inspiration in guiding the family to believe that 'we can do better'."

Wilson said his friend is a "learned man, who can discuss and understand with the best of them. He must read a lot. He is a very bright guy. He is a common sense guy, blessed with intuition and an adventuresome spirit. And, underneath it all, Vince has tremendous values and principles."

Wilson stated that he is amazed at how well the DiCosimo family works together as a unified business entity. "I keep looking for the 'jerk,' the bad brother-in-law, the bad son in-law. I can't find them."

Wilson summed up Vince DiCosimo's incredibly warm and engaging way with people in what Wilson witnessed when Vince and leading international wine merchant, Piero Antinori, of Italy, met recently to discuss business. (The Antinori family has made wine in Italy for 600 years.) Wilson said he was delighted to see Antinori, "a revered world figure, conversing, laughing, joking, having fun and respecting Vincent DiCosimo. It just confirms that Vince's character can be appreciated by every walk of life."

Another of Vince's friends is Dan Patterson, president of Niagara College.

A half century after – and only a few kilometres away from where new immigrants Vince DiCosimo and his brother, Stanley, clasped their shovels to level out a pile of stone in Niagara Falls – Patterson looks across his office's conference table and beams with affection and admiration while discussing Vince and the DiCosimo family.

"They have given a tremendously big gift to this college," said Patterson. "A very special gift. " Patterson begins to reflect on the $500,000 DiCosimo donation and – perhaps something just as delightful to this leading university academic – he talks with pride about his recent and warm friendship with Vince DiCosimo, a scrappy Grade 5 dropout (and Vince would be the first to admit that he lacks formal education.)

Patterson and DiCosimo are two men with the mutual respect of individuals who have worked hard and accomplished much in life, albeit along far different paths. They are also men who know the importance of a hands-on, pragmatic place such as Niagara College.

Patterson noted that the college is not peopled with "elite academics, but we are grounded in the realities of the world." That is the same reality that applies to Vince, a man who knows a thing or two about the hospitality industry – and he didn't learn it from books.

What was the genesis of this friendship between the two men? Well, you might say it was when Vince finally showed up at college. He had a whopper cheque in hand and a growing resolve that it was time to give back to the community, and specifically to the tourism industry that has lavished great gifts on him and on his family.

"I am not an educated man," admits Vince. "But I know how important it (the DiCosimo family's endowment) is, and my grandchildren may go to Niagara College one day."

After Vince DiCosimo announced the gift, his entire family was invited to Niagara College for a meal and to view state-of-the-art cooking facilities, including what will be known as the DiCosimo Family Hilton Fallsview Culinary Theatre. Patterson explained that the DiCosimo gift goes directly toward the college's Futures Ready Campaign, an appeal to raise about $3 million from private enterprise to help fund the school's new, $10-million School of Hospitality and Tourism.

"I think my friend Vince is at a point in his life that he wants to give back," Patterson said. "It's the lovely evolution of (his) personality; he's in a reflective period. We met with Vince and shared with him our literature. He was intrigued by the fact that we were doing this. What really hit me was that Vince has tremendous listening skills. He is intrigued to hear what you have to say on a particular issue. You leave him, after a conversation, feeling that he listened; he identified with what you were saying and was very caring. Vince has a vision and an understanding that transcends just his own self interest and his company's self interest. He knows that the (tourism) industry stands to gain from a strong partnership with Niagara College. At the same time, I think Vince has this sense of legacy around his children and their children. He knows that some of his children's children, and their children, and their children, will be going to Niagara College. Vince wants to leave a legacy. To show them that he stepped up to the plate."

Patterson said that "socially, Vince is just a wonder to watch. He knows how to network, go from table to table, and to make people feel comfortable. He is a role model of what hospitality and tourism ought to be. His communication skills are extraordinary. Vince sees no boundaries in terms of status."

Vince's start in business began – like all beginnings in the bustling commercial world of Niagara Falls – with the sobering question of where, in his new country, he would get money to start in being his "own boss."

The answer can be stated in two words: Sidney Orvitz.

Vince says that Orvitz, an amiable St. Catharines financial wizard, who is still making deals at 84, was really "the key guy" who believed in Vince's early business plans, lent him his first money, and "was always there to help me." The two men became acquainted when Sid's company assumed a house mortgage that Vince had initially taken out with a Niagara Falls resident.

Although Vince no longer relies on Sidney's financial help, they and their families remain good friends. Sid and his wife, Ellen, have travelled and vacationed with Vince and Ida. They've been to Florida, the Bahamas, Chicago, Washington together. Most of these social occasions involved them "sitting around and kibitzing. Vince is a humourous guy."

In Sid's view, Vince has "really not changed" all that much in nearly 50 years. "He is the same Vince that I knew back when he was working in the kitchen."

Sid was impressed from the start with Vince's guts and entrepreneurial spirit. "Vince had sense of 'I can do this. I can do that.' He won't quit. He won't back away from a deal. That is very important. He is down-to-earth. He knows what he wants to do and he does it. He works hard."

Also, and very important to the St. Catharines financier, Vince DiCosimo didn't miss payments. He honoured his obligations. Sid believes that Vince's staying power might be one of the keys to his success.

"Way back then, if he had to be up and in the middle of the night to look after a hotel room, he was there. No problem. At one time all his rooms were rented, so he let people into his own bedroom."

Because Sid believed in Vince, he went to bat for him with banking partners when the Frontier was available for purchase on River Road and Vince wanted to buy it.

"Vince and I discussed it. I spoke to my associates and I told them that I thought Vince was going to make it, that it was a good deal. I told them that this man was really serious about working. Then, The Rapids Tavern was up for sale. Again, the same thing."

Sid believed in Vince. The money came.

When Sid is asked his thoughts about Vince's solid successes in business, he states that "the guy deserves what he has got. He doesn't gamble, he doesn't drink (heavily), he doesn't curse. What else can you ask in a man? He's an all round good guy. He's a good family man."

Ed Lustig was once the solicitor for the City of Niagara Falls and, later, the chief administrative officer. As such, he had official dealings with Vince's businesses. Those transactions developed into friendship. Lustig has known Vince for about 20 years.

"We play golf together," said Lustig. "He's been over to my place for dinner and I've been over to his place. He is a great guy. A very, very nice person. He has very good bones. A great family person. His family is the key to everything. His wife, Ida, is a wonderful lady. His family is the main part of his life."

During the official, municipal dealings that the two men engaged in through the years, Vince was always "direct, forthright, and to the point. He has a nice way about him. He is a very human person. He is able to talk with anyone. He can get through to bank presidents, bureaucrats, politicians, employees. He's got a common touch. Vince's personality is his strong point."

This amiability in no way detracts from his friend's business acumen, Ed observed. He agreed that Vince is "no one's fool. He's made many good deals. That takes savvy."

Even when the city took a position that differed from Vince's business interests, Vince was always "very respectful" of other positions and wasn't "a yeller or screamer or threatener. He was always very co-operative. A very good guy to deal with. One of the best people to deal with."

Mike Manning, the genial server in the hotel's front lobby bar and coffee shop was a Hilton Fallsview "day oner" when the hotel opened seven years ago.

"I have got to say, in all honesty, that this is the best atmosphere that I have ever worked in," said Manning. "The DiCosimos are a great family. They treat you as they would want to be treated themselves. Great family to work for. They never interfere with my job."

Manning, who lives in Niagara Falls, has played golf with Vince DiCosimo. "Vince is a fantastic golfer. He is deadly accurate. He's got a nickname, DTM, "down the middle, 150 yards straight out, every time."

Manning said he is impressed with any man who can rise from being a welder to "slowly progress, through some admirable moves," to owning a first class hotel.

He said Vince, and "the whole family in general" will always take the time to stop by and say hello to employees like him "every day."

Frank DiPalma, president and owner of The Furniture Gallery in St. Catharines, has known Vince and his family for the last five years. Ida and Vince are customers and, more importantly to DiPalma, good friends. He and his wife, JoAnne, chum with them while in Florida.

DiPalma, like Vince, is from a small town in Italy, and came to Canada when he was 19 in 1962, so they have much in common. "Growing up in Italy, from where he came from and where I came from, there is no difference."

"The man is an incredible person," said DiPalma. "He is incredible for his family and friends. He values family, his children, like no others. He talks a lot about his family, his children and his grandchildren. They all are united in what they are doing, in business. Vince is a well-liked person. A very happy person. I have the greatest respect for him. I just don't know anything bad about that man." DiPalma said that Vince is successful in business because he is "an incredible 'people' person" and "you can put down that I said he is a very shrewd businessman. And he has this passion – and his kids are the same."

The St. Catharines businessman, who started out as a barber in Canada, believes that his Niagara Falls friend is "a good example" to all immigrants that hard work and determination leads to success. "He is a setting the wheel in motion for other immigrants."

Donald Ziraldo is the co-founder of Inniskillin Wines and a leader and visionary in Canada's wine industry.

"I got to know the great character and the integrity of Vince DiCosimo while acting in my capacity as chairman of the capital campaign for The Niagara Culinary Institute of Niagara College. Vince and I found a kinship in our love for food, family and friends and, of course, wine. Vince is very interested in wine and he began inviting Italian vintners, like Piero Antinori, Lucio Mastroberardino, and others, to dine with family and friends at winemakers dinners organized at his hotel. I attend a lot of these wine dinners all over the world and I must say Vince knows how to throw a party. We also talked about his vision for a Tuscan-style hotel expansion, architects, his planned golf course and winery. The man has boundless energy.

"I love just sitting and chatting in Italian with Vince over a latte. One of the great stories about Vince is when he was hired by a local contractor in Niagara Falls to drive a truck (recounted elsewhere in this book.)

"We were sitting in his restaurant, The Watermark, one day looking out over the Fallsview Casino. He told me about his first meeting with my friend the chairman, Ron Barbaro, of the Casino Corporation in Toronto, and how, when he realized the new casino would be blocking the view of the Falls from his restaurant. Vince then asked Ron if he could move the building over slightly. And Ron did!

"At one of our many casual meetings Vince said he wanted to help Niagara College build the school's Culinary Institute where one of his nephews was a student. I never mentioned it again. The day I asked Vince, he shook hands with me. Then, he and his family pledged an incredible $500,000 to the campaign. A man of his word.

"On the night of the dedication of the Culinary Theatre, Vince invited his family of 30 plus to the event. Dan Patterson, the college president, surprised Vince by having the grandchildren prepare the dessert for the dinner, in the new kitchen. Vince was beaming as the proud *nonno* and patriarch.

"He should be beaming! He is a man who loves life, is proud of his heritage and supports his community.

"I am proud to call him my friend."

Craig Mance, the head of franchise development for Hilton Hotels for northeast U. S. and Canada, said he has known Vince for the last 10 years.

"He's a wonderful, wonderful man," said Mance. "And, and great family man."

Mance said Vince has "personality, desire and intelligence" and had the good sense to buy a hotel in a "remarkable, remarkable location," right beside the Falls. "My friend Vince had the foresight to realize that rather than having these four or five smaller hotels he'd be better off selling those and concentrating on doing the one Hilton hotel."

Mance confided that the DiCosimo family's present plans to build a 58-storey wing to the present Hilton didn't make him "fall off my chair. What made me fall off my chair was the first time I met with them and they showed me this hotel (Days Inn) that had all of these red, heart-shaped bathtubs and Vince told me he wanted to do a 500-room Hilton. That floored me. But he worked at it and showed us and our architects how he was going to build next to it and over it and he did it."

Mance, 52, said the DiCosimos are a "remarkable family," that makes his own work "a lot of fun." He said the Hilton corporation has great faith in the family because each member of the family is, in his view, professional and hard working. "And they all listen to each other."

He said Vince is "old school" in business "and he reminds me of my own dad, who got out of business because he could no longer do business on a handshake."

"Vince is a very, very trusting guy." And, his word is his bond. And, said the senior Hilton executive, that is good enough for him.

Two years ago, while having dinner at an Italian restaurant in Palm Beach Gardens, Florida, Jim Sardo and his wife, Virginia, met Vince and Ida DiCosimo. Jim and his wife had signed up with Amici d' Italia, a 200-member social club.

Jim's late father, Sam, who died at 90, was born in Italy and like Vince, came to Canada with no education or money. But Sam eventually succeeded in his Toronto shoe repair and shoe-making shop and in a mortgage business.

He said that he was immediately struck with Vince and Ida's "genuine hospitality and friendliness." He said they reminded him of his own relatives. "Vince reminds me a lot of my own dad."

"Vince is a credit to his generation for what he has accomplished," said Sardo, 63, of Mississauga, a university MBA graduate and former CEO and Chairman of Firestone Canada. "Vince is such a genuine person and a hard-working individual. He has a very good set of principles in terms of dealing with people. You cannot match Vince's work ethic. A lot of people work hard, but this is more than working hard in Vince's case; this is personal sacrifice and a dedication to becoming successful."

Sardo said that, like his own mother and father, it seems that Vince and Ida worked in partnership and treated their employees "like they were family."

"I think Vince's business relationships were always on the basis of friendship and credibility and meeting his obligations. There is a tremendous sense of trust in Vince. If he says he is going to do something he does it."

Sardo said that people like Donald Trump, his own father, and Vince, have a certain "vision for opportunity."

These people often see the potential in an investment "that other people cannot see. So when Vince gets a hotel or restaurant he always knew what it could be. To you and me it could have been very risky, but to Vince there was no risk. Vince is a true visionary. He turns a vision into a reality."

"He is a straight shooter. Down the middle on the golf course. And he is very predictable on the golf course and therefore he is predictable in business so bankers put their trust in him."

3

A Boy's Life in San Lorenzo

"I don't know how our mothers put up with us!"

Vincenzo DiCosimo was born to parents Giuseppe and Anna (Sanzari) in San Lorenzo Maggiore, on March 13, 1936.

He was born at home, on Via Forte, and so were his five siblings. The midwife at the time was Rosa Rossi. Attending with Rossi at Vince's birth were Anna's mother, Assunta, and Anna's younger sisters, Rosa and Esterina.

After Rossi retired, the town's midwife was a woman everyone called "Brutta." "She looked like a witch," Vince recalls. "In my own town, when I was a little boy, there were witches. Everybody knew them."

Vince's parents were also born in San Lorenzo, about 70 kilometres northeast of Naples. The 800-year-old town has usually had from 1,500 to 1,800 residents. (San Lorenzo was a Roman martyr executed in 258.) Anne and Giuseppe were married on February 11, 1929 at the Church of San Lorenzo Martire, where Vince was baptized, confirmed, and married.

When he was baptized (always within eight days of any child's birth at that time) Vince's godfather was Libero DiLibero; his godmother was Marietta Iannotti. Baby Vince was given a beautiful gold watch and chain by his godfather. "With large numbers," as Vince remembers. When Vince was set to depart for Canada in 1955, he said his mother gave him the watch that she had put away for safekeeping. To his great regret, Vince misplaced that baptismal watch some years ago.

When Vince was confirmed, at about age 12, his godfather was Antonio Vetrone and godmother was his wife Filomena. (Antonio and Vince's father were prisoners of war together on the island of Ceylon (now Sri Lanka) during the Second World War.)

In that small, town, Vince's older brother, Stanley, ended up marrying Antonio Vetrone's first daughter, Nicoletta. Stanley and Nicoletta live in Niagara Falls today.

Vince and all his siblings, Stanislao (Dec. 20, 1929), Vittorio (April, 20, 1938), Dora (Sept. 20, 1940), Maria (Oct. 8, 1931), and Elena (Sept. 15, 1933) were all born in the large family home on Via Forte in San Lorenzo. Maria, who leaves her husband Nick DiLibero, 78, and children Joseph, John, Patrick, and Nicky, died in Niagara Falls on April 16, 2005 Elena died in Italy on May 2, 2002 Stanley and Nicoletta's children are Joe DiCosimo and Anna Rossi. Dora and Giuseppe's children are Maria and Anna. Vittorio and Maria's children are Anna, Peppino and Rosa.

The DiCosimo farm in San Lorenzo has been in the family for generations. Today, Vince's brother, Vittorio, 69, operates the farm. Vittorio cared for Vince's parents in their senior years.

Vincent was the fourth born. He always felt that his mother "favoured me." His father did too, he thinks.

The family all worked on their large, "self-sustaining" farm, he recalls. They raised wheat, corn, vegetables, grapes, chickens, and pigs. It was a subsistence operation and the only products Vince remembers the family selling for revenue were eggs, olives, and grapes and to the wineries. About 90 per cent of the bounty from the vineyards was sold. The remainder was crushed for Anna's own wine making. Farm revenue was used mostly for clothing and groceries.

"My parents? They worked like slaves. They worked the whole year to harvest at the end of the year. When a hailstorm destroyed the grapes, they never despaired and they always provided for us kids. Maybe they had less wine that year – but they had enough to raise their family and they were always happy."

As stated previously, Anna Sanzari and Giuseppe DiCosimo were both born in San Lorenzo. She on Feb. 7, 1908; he on March 20, 1910. Anne died, at 77, in San Lorenzo on June 30, 1985; Giuseppe died, at 88, in San Lorenzo on April 4, 1998. They are buried in the Cemetery of San Lorenzo Maggiore.

Anna's parents were Mama Maria Assunta Iannotti (1875-1968) and Pasquale Sanzari (1873-1953); Giuseppe's parents were Maria Filomena Manente (1872-1948) and Stanislao DiCosimo (1867-1940).

Although Anna and Giuseppe and their family were not as well off financially as the present generation of DiCosimos, Vince said his parents seemed to live less rushed and stressful lives. They had no mortgages to pay, always enough food on the table, and even with a crop failure, they always knew their luck would change and there would be other crops.

"Have a bottle of wine!" was the announcement when things got a bit rough or just to relax a bit. "Who cares? Tomorrow is another day. Then we go back to work. Raise the grapes, the olive oil, vegetables. That was our life. Over here, there is a lot more pressure than that."

When he was a kid, Vince remembers that his sisters sat in the living room during the evening hours to crochet, "and I used to help them." There was a warming fire in the centre

Vincenzo DiCosimo

Vince's mother, Anna Sanzari, was 20 when this photograph was taken in 1928 in a San Lorenzo Maggiore studio in Italy.

Vince's father, Giuseppe DiCosimo, a tall, hard working farmer, was 18 when this photo was taken at the same studio.

of the room "and everybody got around and everybody had a needle in their hand to do something. I was trying to learn from my sisters, but that didn't last long. Then I went out the door with my friends."

It was really a simple, "dull" life compared with what we all have today, said Vince. No radio, no TV, no car. He doesn't remember a radio until he was about 13. The family sometimes used a horse (a mare named Peppenella) and cart to get around. "But to us, life wasn't dull."

"I was six years old. I had to go to the first grade. I never wanted to go to school. I was scared. I knew I had to write alphabet letters, and I thought 'I cannot do that'. I didn't like school; but I went to school. Two twin cousins of mine dragged me to school. Their parents were not farmers; they were bricklayers, so they were already different (socially) from me. They grabbed me; my head was in the stones. They dragged me. I was crying like crazy."

"I had a woman teacher. (La Signora Casalduni). She taught me for the rest of my education, from the first grade to the fifth. I met her years ago in the square. She was coming out of night school where she taught. I said 'Signora, how are you?' and she said 'Oh, Vincenzo!' She remembered me. It was good. I was glad to see her. She's from my town. She reminded me that my writing was so bad (it still is) that she said it's like chicken scratches. She asked me if my writing ever improved and I said 'You know what, I don't think so, Signora!' I used to sit on the same school bench as her son. I saw him three or four years ago. He's my age and I hadn't seen him since school."

One of Vince's Grade 1 classmates became the chief of police of Naples. "We had to do some work and both of us were trying to copy some homework from a third guy because we didn't do it the night before. The teacher found out what we were doing." She said: "DiCosimo, where's your homework? Put your hand on that desk. And don't move! (She used a piece of wood from the back of a chair for her "strap.") "I put my hand out and when she hit I pulled my hand back and she hit the ink bottle. Ink everywhere. She was like a monster she was so mad."

Vince graduated from Grade 5. That was as far as any of the village children could go. He was 12. "I was happy to finish school. I never wanted to go back."

From the age of 12, to when he left home at 19, Vince worked on the farm and hung out with his pals.

Vince recalls that – with only one parent at home during the war – many of the school children lacked any discipline so the teachers were extra tough. They didn't spare the rod."But we were bad too. All the fathers were in the war. We used to live on the street. I don't know how our mothers put up with us."

Key characteristics of Anna DiCosimo were that she was very generous, hard working and caring. She was also smart and strong-willed. Although she only went to Grade 3, and wasn't a great reader, she "knew everything," said her son. "I think she learned how to write on her own." Her letters to Vince in Niagara Falls were crammed with information. She'd start out writing in big letters, run out of space and then continue the letter around the margins, or anywhere else she could fit in the words. Vince wishes today that he had saved some of those letters.

"In our small town my mother would get into word fights with the neighbours. She would never take criticism from anybody. She would never back down. And she always thought that her kids were the best kids. Nobody would dare criticize her kids.

"I always think that I took after my mother," said Vince. "She always wanted to be a step ahead of the competition. My mother's farmlands (when father was a prisoner of war) were the best looking. She was never happy unless she was first in quality and quantity of stuff she was raising on the farm."

Vince believes his parents spoiled their kids. Mother would shell out money to them, usually on Sunday mornings, but she could also shell out some tough discipline."She used to hit us with a big wooden spoon. Or with a stick – whatever she had in her hand. She would run after me. I'd run around the table to get away from her and she'd tell me to stay put. 'Don't run', she'd say.

"She was also known as a tough cookie in the town. My mother was scared of nothing. Every one in town knew that you had to watch what you say to my mother, because she would tell you off. As a matter of fact, the girls (of the town) were scared to get too close to us kids because of my mother. If she didn't like them (other children), they're done. She would look at the background of the family."

Anna was a good Roman Catholic and believed that good deeds were as important as regular church attendance. "When the Monks came into town to collect for the poor my mother was always there to give to them. She always said that you have to give stuff away because it will always come back to you. She did it because, inside of her, she knew it was a good thing to do."

A crucifix hung over his parents' bed. There were religious prints and artifacts throughout the house. But his mother, a practical person, always criticized the village women who spent two hours in church each day. She wondered how these women ever got any of their work done.

Vincent knows that people throughout the village gave his mother "a lot of credit" for raising her six children, much of the time when her husband was a war prisoner in Ceylon. "She was like a machine. She never got tired. But my mother never really took care of her health, even though she didn't smoke or drink."

Anna was the "winemaker of the house but she never tasted it. She never even tasted a beer. She'd tell me 'You know what? I don't know what it is to be drunk. How does a beer taste'? It's funny, my father, who drank wine, wouldn't even know how to crush the grapes. My mother did everything. My mother loved making wine – it was her passion."

The DiCosimo wine cellar, which exists today in the cold basement of the four-storey home in San Lorenzo Maggiore, held as much as 3,000 litres when Vince was a boy.

"My mother would say 'Peppino (Giuseppe's nickname), taste this, what do you think'?" Peppino always praised his wife's wine.

Vince and his two brothers slept in the same bed. "And this wasn't a king-sized bed either." Some early mornings he and a brother and sister used to climb into their mother's bed. "We'd used to go under the blankets from the top and come out the other end."

All of the children were close to their mother. Vince was perhaps closest to Vittorio, who is younger, "but I was close to my sisters, too. In reality, we were all together. We all used to work together every day on the farm."

His mother relied on Stanley, who was seven years older than Vince, to help her control the other kids. Stan, in turn, would delegate some authority to his siblings. Vince believes that his mother had a soft spot for the girls. "They are women. She would spend more money on my sisters, to dress them up."

Even through the war, his mother always managed to provide a meal before her children went to sleep – even if it was meagre. (They had a productive farm, but soldiers were occupying it and little food could be harvested. One three-acre patch alone was the temporary home of hundreds of Americans.)

"But one night she couldn't get us kids anything – and I reminded my mother of this every time I went back to Italy.

She cooked this black *rigatoni*. I think it was pumpernickel flour. I couldn't stand it. I went to sleep without eating it. We had never seen that before. It never happened again. During the war there was never enough food. We were always hungry."

But when times were better, his mother would simply pick fresh vegetables for supper right from their garden. She even made her own pasta but even that was "a luxury." Usually his mother would mix up three or four vegetables into a type of stew.

The family raised pigs, so there was usually plenty of pork to be eaten. Chickens were kept for eggs, the sale of which brought in petty cash. So, in order to be able to eat some chicken once and a while, Vince admits that he'd break a chicken's leg hoping his mother would have to kill the chicken and it would end up in the cooking pot. "But, you know what she did, she'd put a damned cast on the leg of the chicken. She'd put a little stick and a string around it and the damned chicken would walk again. I used to think that, next time, I've gotta kill the son-of-a bitch."

His mother kept close track of the number of chickens and the number of eggs, Vince recalls. The chickens laid in the coop. But Vince wanted to skim a little cash for himself, so he took one of the best producers and hid the bird in a haystack. "I didn't let her out until she laid some eggs." His mother said she was short some eggs one day and Vince explained to his mother than the hens were probably just getting too old.

Vince used to pick up three or four eggs from this hidden haystack profit centre and have his brother Vittorio take them into town sell for cash. Vittorio also collected eggs under Vince's instructions. "I used to tell Vic what to do. I'd say 'listen, you pick one there and one there and…' This was my own cash business."

How were the boys caught? Well, it involved a neighbour named Maria who liked Vince and Vittorio and offered to "fence" their purloined eggs and sell them along with hers to the broker in town. But one day Vince's mother, Anna, was with Maria at the egg sale (and Maria had quickly hidden the children's' basket) and then the egg buyer said loudly to Maria:

"Hey Maria, where is the kids' basket?" Maria froze and Vince's mother asked "What kids?" The egg buyer answered: "There's a couple of kids here, next door, they are stealing eggs from their mother."

The egg game was over.

"Then," Vince confesses today, "I used to do the olives." He said it was "very common" for farm kids to sell olives to customers, sometimes without their parents knowing about it. His mother suspected that Vince was stealing olives to sell, so she strategically placed toothpicks throughout the olive piles, normally held in big sacks, so that if the olives were disturbed, then the toothpicks would move. "But I knew that, so I got up at two in the morning and took all the toothpicks and scooped from the top," said Vince. Then, he would carefully replace the toothpicks. His father, almost as if he was "covering" for his son's theft, told everyone he felt the olives were merely "settling pretty fast," so it was the right time to make oil. Vince said his mother knew better, and strongly suspected her son of olive theft, which was the fact of the matter. Vince said he had a ready market for the olives and he used the cash to buy cigarettes and espresso.

Vince's father was not bitter when he returned from the prisoner of war camp. He told his family that the English treated him well. "He said they treated him like gold. He ate good food that he could never even get in Italy."

"My father never liked to talk about the war. I always asked him: 'Did you kill anybody?' I wanted to know. Dad always said that he was one of the lucky ones because he was captured and taken to Ceylon because, as soldiers at the time, they were starving to death." (One of Vince's uncles, Vincenzo DiDonato, was captured and imprisoned by the Germans and that was a different story. DiDonato, who died at 95, said the Germans starved and beat prisoners. His uncle, imprisoned for about a year, finally escaped with other prisoners and it took him 20 days to get back to Italy.)

"My father criticized Italy for going to war," recalls Vince. "He said that Mussolini was wrong for getting Italy into the war and said the Italian war leaders should have been ashamed of themselves because they sent these young men to fight but they didn't have rifles to shoot, no food, ammunition, or equipment."

Giuseppe was also hurt that he never received a proper government military pension for the six years taken from his life and given to his country.

In the DiCosimo family, the mother, Anna, had the "business mind," and handled the money, said her son. She also had opinions on the running of the farm which she expressed to Giuseppe; but Vince can't remember them ever fighting over anything. Anna was also a hard worker, who never quit until the job was finished and "I am like that," said Vince.

Anna's strong ambition, Vince believes, came from the successful Sanzari family, who were well off then, and now. She was also a generous woman who gave much to the poor in the town.

"She always told me that, in life, you have to give away things. You have to give to people who need it most."

Vince still recalls the pride he had in having his mother travel to the nearby town of Benevento to buy him a sharp pair of blue pants and a white shirt. He still favours blue pants today – but he's switched to dark shirts.

Vince and his brother and sisters were born and and raised in this four-storey home on Via Forte in San Lorenzo Maggiore. His brother Vittorio and his family now live there and run the DiCosimo family farm. This is a painting of the large, old dwelling.

Anna liked her children to be with "quality" people, said Vince, and was particular about whether or not various boyfriends and girlfriends were good enough to be with her offspring.

In Italy it was "very common" for spouses to hold different political views. Anna was a liberal; her husband was a democrat who felt that "politicians were a bunch of crooks." But Vince does not recall the two ever having political debates in the house.

"They got along. Sometimes there were little arguments, but minor stuff." (Well, he does recall that dad was "really upset" with mom when he thought he got locked out of the house one late night because he couldn't find the hidden key. "He thought that my mother had locked him out; he woke everybody up." Vince explained that someone had simply forgotten to hide the key.)

With six children, and all alone when her husband was a prisoner of war, Anna DiCosimo was a good and hardworking housekeeper who also had to run a farm. Her cooking was "fairly good" and "basic." Vince particularly remembers her making delicious pork sausages during community cooking sessions when other women would pitch in after a pig was killed. It took about a week to process every part of the pig.

The DiCosimo girls helped in the kitchen. The eldest daughter, Maria (who died in 2005 at 74), was a better cook than their mother, according to Vince. His mother always dished out the food and varied the portions. The DiCosimo kids, as all kids do, scolded mom for giving someone else more food. "My mother always treated my little sister, Dora, differently and we used to complain. How come Dora gets more than me? She's your favourite!"

Mealtimes were orderly. "There was no reason to shout – everybody was concentrating on the food."

His father, Giuseppe – called "Peppino" not only by his wife but by just about everybody else in town – was a happy and easy-going man. Also, he was a good farmer. "He didn't look for anything else when he came back from the war. He just wanted to go to work. He loved farming. For him, that was all there was to life. He left before daylight and always came home after dark."

In his last years he still did not use eye glasses, was a bit hard of hearing "what he didn't want to hear," and still read the news about the government's agricultural policies. He always argued that the American market had to be opened up to Italian wine. "He said that when America starts to drink wine, that's when we are going to make money and, you know what? He was right."

In his younger years, Giuseppe used to gamble quite a bit in the local cantina. The men would play a traditional Italian hand game involving fingers and the shouting out of numbers. They played for wine. From four to six men were in it at a time. They played for control of the wine, and some of them got drunk. "It was so fast," said Vince. "They used to have a lot of fights. It wasn't a question of really gambling; it was more drinking. I used to remember fights on the street, brother against brother with long knives and chasing each other just because something went wrong in the game."

He can't recall his father in a fight and he can't really remember him being drunk "although he loved wine. And he never touched (hurt) my mother."

Vince recalls that his father, who retired when he was about 69, always worked from dawn to dusk, came home, washed up, and sat down at the table. He was a slow eater. "He spent a lot of time at the table. Maybe it would take him an hour and a half, or two hours. After, he'd continue to drink wine and smoke his clay pipe, using his strong tobacco, and my mother was always complaining about that

San Lorenzo Maggiore in the province of Benevento, Italy. It is a small, hillside town which usually has a population ranging around 1,500 to 1,800. Its ancient buildings are surrounded by farms. The town is about 70 km. northeast of Naples.

pipe. 'Stop smoking that, I can't stand it'." she'd say. "'Why don't you go outside'?"

Vince made the stems for his father's pipe out of bamboo."My father would ask me to make him bent ones, straight ones, and lots of them so that he could always change them around. I used to be very handy." (Today, in Niagara Falls, Frank DiCosimo has some of his grandfather's pipes.)

Giuseppe DiCosimo, who always claimed he never inhaled the pipe smoke, feared missing any single opportunity to smoke so much that he stashed his pipes in various places all across his farm properties, said Vince. For many years Vince sent his father American pipe tobacco from Florida. He'd send about 10 packs every six months. Giuseppe considered any arrival of those vacuum-packed parcels from his son to be a grand occasion. The old man would spread all of his various brands of American tobacco out on a table and ceremoniously mix it in with some other tobacco he had. Then, when Giuseppe stoked up his pipe with American tobacco "the whole town knew it. The aroma was all over."

Vince said that one time an empty box arrived at the DiCosimo house in Italy and his dad "was going crazy" because he figured that the authorities were wise to his tobacco-exporting son and they would soon be arresting Vince. Vince said he made sure after that incident that all of the tobacco was vacuum packed and that packages of tea surrounded it.

His father came to Canada when Vince and Ida were involved in their first businesses, but he never saw his son's many hotels and restaurants. "He said, 'listen, I love everything you guys did, but I'll never come back here.' "He was very happy for us, but he just wanted to be back on the farm. My mother, she was the business woman, wanted to know everything (about the DiCosimo ventures) and I told her." However, Anna DiCosimo died at 76, about 20 years ago, without seeing what her son and his family had managed to build in Niagara Falls.

His father always complained that grape growers didn't get enough money for their produce.

The family worked side by side with father, a farmer who was "well respected in the town."

"We were workers. We all worked together with my sisters. The whole day. My mother used to bring the food. It was like having a picnic every day. My mother always brought a bottle of wine for father." In the farm field his father was "very careful with us, he never pushed us." They took breaks when it was hot. "Two or three o'clock in the afternoon he'd say 'you guys okay'?" Sometimes they would stop at 10 a.m. because of the heat and his father would tell them to rest under a tree. "He was very careful. He never pushed us." His mother was more capable of pushing the kids to work harder. "She was the aggressive type."

Vince became quite good at grafting grapevines. "I used to love to do it." But he can remember catching hell once from his dad when he grafted some wrong vines, a total mismatch. Work was from dawn to dusk, and Vince always knew that being a farmer would never be for him.

Another way to get out of work for awhile was to tell his dad that, because Anna DiCosimo had not yet shown up with the lunch for the workers, he would scoot down to the house and pick it up. "I'd say, listen, I'm going to go and see if maybe mother might have had an accident."

He and his brother Vittorio used to spend summer nights out in the fields in a small, garage-like building their father had constructed. Their job was to watch the animals and the crops. "People were stealing. Everybody was stealing." Vince was afraid of the dark. "When the darkness came, my heart was like… well, the sky was coming down on me."

Vince also used to sneak off at night on occasion and head down to the village centre, but he had to watch out that he didn't meet up with his father in town when he was supposed to be on guard duty out in the field.

In the daytime, his father used to bring lunch out to Vince and Vittorio at their watch station building. "But I used to say 'ma, that's not fair' I want to eat with you, with the family. I don't care who is going to watch the chickens. I want to come home and eat and then I will go back."

Father would also, on occasion, arrive unannounced, and sit outside the guard building on a big stone and smoke his pipe. "My father wanted to make sure that his boys were safe. We were two young kids out there alone. My father would come to check us at two in the morning. We didn't even know he was there."

Then, there was the famous corn incident.

An older neighbour boy, who was about 15, got Vince and his brother into big trouble with the suggestion that they all steal some corn from a neighbouring farm and hold a corn roast. Naturally, the older lad, who "brainwashed" the brothers, suggested that Vince (about nine years old at the time) and Vittorio go and take the corn while he would act as the lookout. The brothers stole the corn, got the fire going, and then the owner (who happened to be the uncle of the future Ida DiCosimo) showed up and the lads "almost collapsed" with fright. The older boy had long since run away. Vince tried to stall for time by telling the farmer that it was DiCosimo corn that was being roasted.

Vince recalls that it was a sunny day in the village piazza and his father was there chatting with his circle of friends when the farmer showed up with the evidence – the stolen corn.

"Here, Peppino, look, here's what your kids have done!" said the farmer in front of about 20 of his father's closest friends. "This is the work of your kids." Vince's father said very little to the accusing farmer but he rushed home and took Anna with him to go out and punish the boys. He got his two sons together and Vince knew they were in for a beating. Vince valiantly told his brother that he'd stand in front of Vittorio to try to protect him from dad. "I'll take everything," Vince promised his brother. "I'll take the punishment."

Meanwhile, his mother was so concerned that her husband was going to harm the kids and she stepped in. Vittorio ran, and dad grabbed hold of Vince, led him to a tree, and threw a rope over it.

"Where did you get that corn?" Giuseppe demanded.

"What corn?" Vince answered. "Are you for real? Do YOU want to hang?" Giuseppe, angry with Vince's smart remarks, wrapped the rope around Vince's neck. "My mother was going nuts!"

Vince managed to unwrap the rope and run away.

Forgiveness was always out of the question over the corn incident, and Vince said he "felt very bad" about shaming the family. His dad, a proud and respectable man in the region, never again talked about the theft by his boys – even to joke about it with the family. "My father was a very strict and respectable man. But my mother never forgave that farmer who insulted her husband (with the accusations) in front of my father's friends."

The only thing that rankled the young Vince about his easy-going father was that the family always was forced to wait until he came back from the fields to eat the evening meal. Vince wanted dinner over with so he could get back out and play with his friends.

"But he wouldn't show up. We could never have supper until he was at the table. I used to complain to my mother that I couldn't put up with that. I said to mother that you have got to tell him that he's got to come home a little earlier." His mother finally asked because Vince said he wouldn't dare.

"What do they wait for me for?" his father answered when he heard the request. "Tell them to eat."

Although Giuseppe was an easy-going man, and Anna was usually the disciplinarian, dad could nevertheless lay down the law with his kids on occasion.

Like during the tomato skin incident.

Unlike today, in those days tomato sauce usually contained the skins of the tomatoes and "I could not swallow the damned things," Vince explains. So, on one memorable occasion he just spit out the skins while he was sitting with the family at the Sunday dinner table.

"I'll never forget it. My dad sat almost across from me. He was big, tall. Well, he slapped me across the face so hard for spitting. 'What the hell are you doing'?"

Vince's father had a "lot of friends. They liked him. He was respected. He was a solid, good man. He did his business; he didn't bother anybody."But his father was also no fool and would stick up for himself if things got rough in the cantinas during games and wine drinking there.

Giuseppe was not a big fan of priests, his son admits today. The farmer, who didn't attend church, didn't think the clergy had much to tell him. He also figured all politicians were liars. His mother Anna, was religious, regularly attended church, and so did the children. "My mother made sure we all went to church. After school we went to prepare ourselves for the first communion. That was all my mother's work. My father didn't care. He went to work and that's it."

When he wasn't in school or working on the farm, Vince's boyhood seemed to be spent hanging out in the local cafes and going to the movie house to see American films. At the cafes, the young teenagers bummed cigarettes, or stole the odd puff of a smoke from someone's ashtray, drank coke or espresso, played cards, and watched the adults.

As in any small town anywhere in the world, Vince hung around with "three or four" close friends, as did others in their own age groupings. He noted that two of them, heavy smokers, have since passed on. He still stays in touch with many in the village because he and family members visit often.

To this day, when Vince hears the peal of church bells it reminds him of that simple and happy time in the village and his family farm.

The greatest thrill for the village kids was going to the afternoon (American) movies. John Wayne, Tyrone Power, Tex Ritter, Clark Gable. Because the American actors' voices were craftily dubbed over with Italian voices, Vince said he usually thought his screen heroes were Italians. "The fun for us at that time was the movies. That was our life. But we didn't have the money to go." Lack of the admission price never stopped Vince and his pals from entering the theatre. One kid would pay the admission price, enter the film house, and then open the fire exit door to let his friends in.

He'd also tell the owner of the local theatre, Filomena, that he wanted to see a particular movie, but he didn't have any money. "I'll pay you tomorrow" Vince would promise. So, Filomena would mark it down. Vince would run up a bill. But Filomena also had a grocery store, so when Vince's mother went shopping Filomena would say: "Anna, there is a little account here..."

Mum paid.

When he and his pals took a short hike out of town to another movie house, Vince would tell that theatre owner his father's name, and said his dad would make up the admission price. "My dad couldn't care less." And he never showed up to pay his son's debt, Vince admits.

The kids tried to get to the movies every week. They begged, borrowed, or asked for credit for the admission price. "Whatever it took to see a movie!"

The *Confetti* Kids – San Lorenzo children, and Vince says he's in this photo somewhere, scramble for *confetti* (little candies) that are thrown out along each wedding procession. Vince believes he was about seven at the time and he can recognize a few relatives and friends in the photo.

The swashbuckling Tyrone Power, at the height of his career, was Vince's particular favourite. He also loved the opera movies that were popular then. Vince still loves the opera, his favourite being *Il Travatore*. "I used to learn all the words. When we came out of the movies we used to go and sing the opera all over town. I know them all. When I was working on the farm I would sing opera."

(The Italian-made movie, *Cinema Paradiso*, released about a decade ago, is a particular favourite of Vince and Ida's. It reminds them of their youth in Italy. The couple has seen the film at least five times.)

Stanley, seven years older than Vince, who was then 6, took his little brother to the La Guardia movie house in the next town for first time. Vince, the film house novice, continued to stare at the projection booth, waiting for the action to start, until Stan informed his brother to look the other way – at the screen.

When the kids weren't watching their movie heroes, they also witnessed some real life action from time to time, when some toughs, too young to have been conscripted into the Italian army, would have too much *vino* at the local *cantina* and take after each other with knives.

As in his youth, his village, like most others in Italy, still stages a feast on the first Sunday in June when the Madonna is paraded about town and out into the countryside. (The other feast is on August. 10.) The celebrations last several days. People would donate money to the Madonna and it was collected in the parade.

Vince's mother would give him a 10,000 lire bill to donate to the Madonna, he recalls. Village men would march with a big banner, stretched across big poles, and you would pin you donations on the banner. But Vince admits that he would keep the 10,000 lire and offer up a 1,000 lire bill to the men. "I would say to the men 'hey, are you going to put a name to that (1,000 lire bill)?" They said no, and Vince knew he was safe. If the 1,000 lire was identified as having come from the DiCosimo family, "my mother would have gone nuts." Vince said he never had the nerve to tell anybody about the 9,000 lire "misappropriation" until he was much older.

"The reason I remember that celebration is that every parent, the ones who could afford it, wanted their children to dress up." His family, being "upper middle class," could afford it so Vincent, about 10 then, was asked what he wanted to wear and he said: 'Ma, I need blue pants and a white shirt.' I dressed up. I was so proud."

An orchestra was set up in the town square. Friends from other towns were invited. Every home would put out wine and food. Most of the women stayed home to cook while the Madonna was paraded about.

He recalls that his mother placed "beautiful velvet blankets" over the balcony windows, as most families did, out of respect for the Madonna. The girls of the town carried baskets of flowers that they scattered on the streets.

At Christmas, the family attended church but he can't remember the exchanging of gifts. On Christmas morning his mother would give each child some money, the amount depending on the age of the child. The older ones got more, as Vince recalls. At Epiphany, January. 6, each kid got an orange and an apple in a sock if you "were good." If you were bad you'd get a piece of charcoal.

Vince believes that he was probably "the bad one in the family. I was a little different. I always stole stuff from my mother. And every time she found out something about me she'd promise to kill me."

He said he can still hear his mother's footsteps on the stairs coming up to the boys' bedroom to spank him. If he was in bed with Vittorio, he'd quickly put his brother on top of him so that his mother, in the unlit bedroom, would start whacking at Vittorio thinking she was punishing Vince.

"My brother would yell 'what did I do'?"

In their younger days, Vince was very close to Vittorio as he remains today – telephoning his younger brother often on the farm in Italy. He has fond memories of Vittorio. They were quite different boys.

"Vittorio used to be very careful with money," said Vince. "I never was. Whatever money my mother would give him, he used to save it. He used to hide it all over the house. For some reason I always needed money and I would ask him for money. He would say no. I would ask him where he hid it, but he wouldn't tell me.

"My eyes used to take me to the money." For instance, in his mother's bedroom there was a marble top to one of her dressers, and Vince looked under it to find some of his brother's money.

"So, I took a little bit; Hey, I didn't take it all."

4

A Boy's Life in San Lorenzo (Part Two)

"God's watching that horse."

In San Lorenzo, while Vince was growing up, rich people lived on walled estates. Each of these families had fine gardens of four or five acres. "They had people working in them; it was the place for wealthy people to relax." These days, Vince and Ida, after a lifetime of hard work, themselves employ people to work in their own garden at their luxury home in a "gated" community in Florida. Many early mornings, talking on his cell phone in his Florida yards as a groundskeeper trimmed hedges, the Niagara Falls businessman's remarkable memory transported him back to his birthplace in Italy.

Vince recalls clearly the strange women whom the people in San Lorenzo believed were actual witches. "Everybody knew them. There was one witch that every time I came from the farm or school I had to go by her house. She'd always sit on these damned stone steps. And she would go: 'Did you bring me anything today?' I said 'no.' 'Well, you had better watch out!' she said. I told my mother. My mother went to that woman and said: 'Listen, if you ever touch my kid, I will kill you'!" Vince said he never believed in witches but his grandfather always told some chilling stories about them.

As kids in San Lorenzo, the DiCosimo kids didn't have the store-bought toys and electronic games that are enjoyed by children today. However, Vince remembers with fondness his first bicycle. It belonged to his godfather, Antonio Vetrone, who sold it to his mother for about 6,000 lire ($4).

"It was a dream come true. I never rode a bike before."

Vince, who was 13, learned on that full-sized bike. But when it got a flat tire, he had no money to fix the tube. So he stuffed the wheel with hay. As can be imagined, bicycles were difficult to navigate on stone roads. "I tied it all up with a piece of string and that's the way I rode it. It was my first and last bike. At the end it finally broke down. I could not afford the tubes. I never rode another bike."

He recalls also making a little wooden car with a rope to control the front-wheel steering. "Me and my younger brother, Vittorio, wanted to get something on wheels. It was like a buggy; he'd push me down the hill."

At about the time he got his first bicycle he took lessons at the local church for his confirmation in the Roman Catholic Church. He recalls one time that a local merchant stopped his horse and carriage at the front of the church. Some of the children, who were attending the religious classes with Vince, asked the man if he was going to leave the horse there alone. "The guy told the children 'don't worry, God will take care of it'."

That night, as Vince was with the priest deep into a lesson with the other children, the priest asked the children whether or not anyone could tell him where God was located. "I know! I know!" yelled one kid. "He's outside watching that horse."

Vince said that his life as a child in San Lorenzo was enriched by his friendship with his favourite aunt, Maria Iannotti, who led a somewhat troubled life. Maria was his father's sister and she lived nearby. (Vince's father did not discuss his own sister but he insisted Maria be brought plates of food from the DiCosimo home and cared for in other ways.)

Everyone called her "Mariuccia." (Italians are fond of using terms of endearment.) In her younger years, Maria pitched in and helped on his family's farm, said Vince. Maria's husband, Vincenzo, had deserted her and moved to America, so she eased this, and some of life's other disappointments, with wine. Giuseppe gently warned Vince not to bring her wine with the meals the family provided. But Vince, independent as usual, didn't listen because he knew what his favourite aunt really wanted, perhaps needed.

But even Vince had to be careful of the amount of wine he would sneak over to his aunt's house. "Whatever you would give her, she would drink it." When his parents were away, he would allow Maria into the family wine cellar. But then he would caution her "drink whatever you want, but don't stay more than 10 minutes, somebody is going to show up. I would knock on the cellar door and say 'are you done'? I felt sorry for my aunt Maria. She was such a nice lady. I always wondered why this woman lived alone."

Vince liked Maria because she told him stories about his grandfather and grandmother DiCosimo. "She knew everything." His favourite aunt would also help Vince cover up the fact that he sometimes skipped school. Sometimes he would drop off his books at her home, play all day with his friends, and then pick up his books at his aunt's place just after school was let out, and then walk home.

Music and dancing were always a big part of life in San Lorenzo. Marriages, baptisms and other celebrations called for local musicians to be called to homes "and the kids would find out where these houses were and we'd sneak in – but you had to know the family."

Vince said he used to like the dances, "because that's where the girls were. But I was a little troublemaker and a lot of times I'd be told 'you are not welcome'."

Usually there was only one man, Vittorio Barbato, who provided the music for these festivities, with his accordian. Vince was continually rejected entry to these parties so he figured that if he bought Barbato's accordion then he would "control the music" and couldn't be denied entry.

"The families were almost forced to call me," said Vince, who could never play the accordion. He eventually got another guy to play the instrument – but Vince still controlled the music.

His grandmother, Assunta, loved Vince's accordion playing, bad as it was, and promised to buy him a new one if he truly learned to play. Vince couldn't even read music, but neither could his grandmother, although "she loved the sound." Grandmother eventually bought Vince a new accordion in Naples because he promised her that when he went to Canada, and he had some time, he'd take lessons and be able to play well. Vince took the new accordion to Canada. It was a "Paulo Soprano" model, Vince recalls, the best available in Italy. "I figured if the worst came to the worst (in Canada) I could always sell it."

At the time, when he was living in Niagara Falls at his brother Stanley's apartment, Vince felt that playing the accordion well would be his ticket to any party of social event in the city, "but gradually I lost interest" and he sold the Paulo Soprano for $75 to his sister-in-law's brother, Rito Vetrone, who became a musician. (Vetrone, a younger man, is today a doorman at a Niagara Falls casino, and he and Vince are friends.)

But Granny's accordion is long gone.

5

War Comes to Vince's Town

"You make another move and you are dead!"

To a small boy in a small Italian town, The Second World War was a confusing but thrilling time.

The fatherless DiCosimo family struggled for survival – as did the many other fatherless families in San Lorenzo Maggiore. Captured by the British Army in Abyssinia, Vince's father, Giuseppe, was held in a prisoner of war camp in Ceylon (now Sri Lanka) for six years.

Highly censored letters from him arrived every six months, or so, and his family wrote back. (Some letters to Giuseppe were routed more quickly with the help of a Canadian soldier, remembered only as "Carlo," who mailed them to his mother back in Canada, and she sent them onward to Giuseppe in Ceylon, an island country just off the southeast coast of India.)

During those long six years, Anna DiCosimo and the children struggled to operate the San Lorenzo farm, just to get enough to eat. The family also had to contend, first of all with the occupying German forces, and then, after the liberation, to get along with the Americans, Canadians and English who occupied their land.

To Vince the war was "an adventure." But it was also dangerous, as it was for everyone in his town. On two occasions, Vince escaped death or serious injury. Another time, both he and his brother were badly injured.

Vince recalls those incidents with the thankfulness of any survivor: A German soldier might have shot him; a British soldier could have punched him out, or worse; and a dynamite cap nearly killed him and his brother and their friend in a horrible explosion.

By pulling the trigger, the German soldier could have ended it all right there. He would have snuffed out the life of a rambunctious Italian kid.

The year was 1943. Vincent was a feisty seven-year-old. He was as confused about why the two German soldiers were standing in his maternal grandparents' home on that day in San Lorenzo as he was about why his father had been taken away from him. Vince was at the Sanzari residence with his mother and two sisters. The German soldiers were scrounging for food and they knew there was food in the home.

"They got everybody outside and we were on a patio. This younger German, a little thin guy, was waving the gun, and the other guy goes to look for food. The guy with the gun put me, my mother and my grandpa, and other members of the family, against the wall."

His grandfather, about 70, got tired and had to drop his arms. So the German smacked the old man with his rifle. "My poor grandfather. I jumped on this soldier to throw him off. I wanted to choke him. This guy turned and threw me right against the wall. Then he picked me up and put the gun to my head. He said 'You make another move and you are dead.' My mother, omigod, she almost died."

And so did Vince DiCosimo.

But the Germans eventually left, "and we went on with our lives. Everybody in town usually locked themselves in the house and tried not to walk around in the streets too much."

Vince DiCosimo did not realize it then, but he realizes it now, that many of the German invaders – with their supply lines stretched thin all across Europe – were probably just as hungry as the struggling Italian villagers whose land they were occupying. "They didn't have too much food themselves. They were starving themselves. So they used to go around to families like us and if we had a pig, they'd take it. A chicken, whatever. They had to feed themselves, but it made it harder for us."

Then, there was the day, during those war years, that Vince and his brother, Vittorio, were nearly killed. It was a rainy day. The brothers took shelter under the arch over the "portone" of the family home. With them was an 18-year-old lad, Elvio Mastanduono, who had found a blasting cap and foolishly asked the brothers if they had a match to light the cap. Vince had a large wooden match and he gave it to Elvio. That lad positioned himself between the two brothers and ignited the cap that was resting on the door ledge.

"Since that day, I cannot hear noises without jumping," explains Vince about the cap's detonation.

As the cap blew, Vince managed to place his hands in front of his face and this surely helped saved him from more serious injury. When he opened his hands in the next split second, Vince saw a horrible sight that he remembers to this day: he watched the hand of Elvio fly into the entranceway and strike a horse cart.

"I then looked at my brother and he was dark, his face was like charcoal. He was blinded. I was also hurt and I had blood all over me. I was like the Passion of Christ."

It took the two brothers about six months to heal at the family home. "We were so sick we couldn't even talk." Mother put both of her boys in her bed while they recovered.

At the time of the explosion, Vince's mother was visiting her parents about a mile away. However, Stanley, his older brother, heard the explosion and he ran toward the home.

He found his brother, Vittorio, lying on the ground and picked him up and carried him to the home of Dr. Iadanza.

Meanwhile, Vince, blood pouring from him, had walked away from the accident scene. Because he was likely in shock, and probably in a proud child's state of denial, Vince admits now that he didn't seem to think much of what had just happened. A woman neighbour, Lucia, saw the bloody boy and asked what happened and Vince said he was "just going for a walk in the town."

"No! No!" yelled Lucia. "You are going to die! Let me clean you up." She quickly wiped him down with warm water and got him to the doctor's home. Elvio was already there as was Vince's mother and his grandmother, Filomena, who eventually ended up with Vince on her lap, moving his legs to try to ease the pain in them.

Eighteen-year-old Elvio, instigator of the accident, was taken away by the American Red Cross and underwent an operation on his arm. "I lost track of him and I always wondered what happened to him." Then, about 10 years ago, Vince met him in Italy. Mastanduono was a university professor and he had an artificial hand. "He said to me, Vincenzo, do you remember me? I never had a chance to apologize. I heard you are doing well in Canada. I'm happy! I never saw Elvio again."

While the boys were recovering from their injuries, Dr. Iadanza, the village's only physician, would come to visit the DiCosimo home every morning. "It was wartime, and everybody was starving, including the doctor's family. He had four daughters and no food. So my mother, to make sure he looked after us properly, always would get a basket of food for him. And he would say 'Anna, no, you've got more kids than I have'."

Vince's problem was that bones from Elvio's shattered hand had lodged in his legs and the doctor had to dig the splinters out or infection would set in. "That hand, when it left the arm of Elvio, disintegrated," said Vince. "And all of those little bones were in my leg, right down to my foot. The doctor never put me to sleep but he took those bones out."

Placed on the dining room table for the morning operations, Vince would swear and scream and call the doctor names – which greatly upset Vince's mother. "He was going to hurt me. My mother was apologizing to the doctor, but the doctor said, 'Anna, let him call me whatever he wants. I have got to get those bones out of his legs or this guy is going to die of gangrene '."

The doctor would slice into the legs and then place the tiny bone splinters on a little plate and show it to Anna DiCosimo every morning that he operated. "I still have the scars."

Dr. Iadanza confided in Anna that her boys were lucky that he had access to American penicillin to administer to them because, without it, gangrene would surely have set in.

After two months, Vittorio DiCosimo still could not see. The doctor felt that Vittorio was too young to be operated on and felt that his sight might come back by itself in due time. The doctor said they had to "wait for a miracle." That miracle happened. Within about six months Vittorio regained his sight, although he still had metal fragments from the blasting cap lodged in his face. The doctor couldn't pull them out and Vittorio – who now runs the DiCosimo farm in San Lorenzo – still has those fragments lodged in his face.

If the boys were not blowing themselves up they – and everyone else in the village – were always in danger of being blown up by bombs from above. A truck with a loudspeaker would roll around through town warning everybody to head out to the countryside because the village might be soon be attacked.

His mother's parents lived near the edge of town in a house built on a huge rock. Underneath was a cave. When the German soldier showed up, his mother took the family to her parents' place to hide in the cave.

"We'd sit there for a couple of days and then another voice (loudspeaker) comes around, all over, and says that everybody's got to move into town because they are going to bomb the farms. I wasn't scared. But I guess my mother was."

The schoolteachers, on many occasions, would rush the children from classes when there was a threat of a bombing. The school would close and the children told to get home.

For a young street kid, like Vince, the war was fun. In addition to his own father, every other man in his village had been called up into the Italian army. So, the fatherless kids ran wild in the streets and across the countryside. "We were pretty bad. I was rough, but I was like everybody else. We would never listen to our mothers."

Vince recalls vividly the day the Americans liberated his village.

"There was word that the Americans were close. All of a sudden there was this big noise. Omigod, all of us kids we were so happy! I was right there. The Germans had left just two days before. It was the best day of our lives."

The Italian kids would chase the Yanks around hollering "Cica! Cica!" (Gum! Gum!) There would usually be one American, on the back of some jeep, holding a single pack of gum out to "about 50 kids" running like a wild pack of wolves behind. "He'd yell 'come on and get it!' We nearly all killed each other. We all tumbled after him. It was going about 50 miles an hour. We were all scratched up for some lousy gum."

Vince remembers that his mother, who was no doubt influenced by whispers about the Holocaust, didn't want her family using bars of soap because she suspected it was made from human flesh. "She was worried about that."

His mother warned her children about picking up anything on the ground, fearing they would be killed or injured by explosives or booby-trapped articles like pens, lighters – or even hand grenades shaped like potatoes.

When the Allies finally drove the German occupiers away from Vince's village, the children found a new occupation. They begged for candy and smokes from the soldiers of the liberation forces.

Vince recalls that the British seemed to drink quite a bit, and the Canadians "were the best. They were more family - oriented and acted more like gentlemen."

Despite warnings from parents, the kids would scrounge about the countryside looking for ammunition and, on one winter occasion, two boys brought some live rounds into the schoolhouse and tossed them into the stove while the teacher wasn't looking. When the ammo went off, the teacher was injured and Vince remembers escaping out a schoolhouse window and landing about 10 feet down on the roof of a neighbouring house.

From an early age, Vince always had a fascination with big machinery. So, when he saw the wonderful American Army tanks, he scampered off to see if he could climb aboard. "I told my mother I was going to school but, instead, I would go away from the town to look at these army tanks. There must have been 50 of them, all lined up behind one another. I wanted to see how they worked."A nervy kid, Vince would jump right onto a tank and drop right in through the hatch.

"What the hell are you doing in here?" the American soldiers would scold him in English. The truant schoolboy, who was about seven or eight years old, would jump from tank to tank. When he returned to school later in the morning he'd confess to his teacher that he'd been out looking at the U.S. Army tanks.

Americans, and later Canadian soldiers, who camped out on the DiCosimo farm property, would sometimes invite family members to eat with them in their tents.

"They were part of us."

The Canadian soldier named Carlo, the son of Italian immigrants in Canada, spoke some Italian and was a favourite with Vince. But Carlo was soon called with his regiment to attack Monte Cassino. The young Canadian came to the DiCosimo family and said "Listen, I don't think I am going to come back." Carlo wrote a letter to his mother and asked the DiCosimos to make sure she received it.

Monte Cassino, a mountaintop monastery, was about two hours from San Lorenzo Maggiore. The battle that ensued against the Germans entrenched atop the mountain, turned into a bloodbath. Carlo was a paratrooper and the DiCosimos heard that Carlo and his entire regiment were all shot dead while they were parachuting in for the attack.

British paratroopers soon showed up in the village. They liked to drink. "They were there to rest before going somewhere, so they liked to eat and drink," said Vince.

Vince would wash dishes for the British and be paid with packs of cigarettes which he stashed away in a metal munitions box that the boy had "liberated" from the Allies. Vince didn't smoke at the time, but he loved the look of all the cigarette packs in his munitions box. He knows that his older brother, Stan, who already was smoking, stole as many as he could from his kid brother.

One time he was promised payment by a British soldier if he did the dishes. The soldier was drinking. "It was a green bottle of beer," Vince recalls now. "I said I wanted a bottle of beer; I don't want a pack of cigarettes. So, when I finished I said 'where's my beer?'"

The Brit offered the boy his empty bottle.

Vince said he was "hurt" by this gesture. "He was teasing me." So the farm boy grabbed the bottle and smacked the soldier over the head with it. He somehow escaped being assaulted by the soldier. Vince was told later, by another soldier, that "I did the right thing. All I know is that I had done the dishwashing."

About a year after his two sons had been injured by the blasting cap, Giussepe DiCosimo, then 36 years old, returned home from the war. "We didn't know when Dad was coming back. One early morning, I recall, this guy came in and said 'Where's your mother?' and I said she's in there making the bed and he said to me: 'Vince, your father is home'! My father had come home and stopped at his friend's house; he didn't want to surprise us. Me and my brother, Vittorio said, right away: 'C'mon, let's go get him'. So we walked with this guy 10 kilometers and I met my father."

Vince said he doesn't remember if he could recognize his dad at the time, "but I guess when I saw him I knew he was my father."

Vince remembers that his dad looked at his brother, Vittorio, whose face was still darkened by the imbedded metal fragments, and said to his son: "Hey, why didn't you wash your face this morning? My brother started to cry." Vince said he stepped in right away and told his father about the blasting cap accident.

"It looks like you two boys fought the war here, also," said Giuseppe DiCosimo. His dad, and his two boys, walked back to the town. Giuseppe's friends flocked to the home and while no one was looking, Vince had a peek into his dad's luggage. He found "this beautiful can" of what the boy thought was tobacco. By that time, Vince was about 10 years old and he was smoking.

Vince rolled some smokes with the stolen "tobacco" from the "beautiful can." It was India tea and not a very good smoke. "We had never seen tea in our lives," he said.

His father told the family that even though he was imprisoned for six years, "we were the lucky ones because we were the prisoners of the English, who never threatened them. They fed us well. We were the big shots. They treated the prisoners like human beings. The camp was clean. They had good food. My father loved that island (Ceylon). He talked about it."

He said his father and the other Italian prisoners worked on tea plantations in the fertile fields of the British colony.

"That's where my father learned to drink tea."

6

Leaving Italy

"I arrived in Niagara Falls with a dirty face."

Even back then – in the world of carefree village street life in San Lorenzo Maggiore – Vince knew, deep in his heart: "I was different from the other kids. I knew that I couldn't farm with my father forever. I didn't like it. I always told my mother I wanted to be a lawyer. I thought I had enough brains to be a lawyer."

He realized that somewhere other than Italy would be where his fortune would be made. When he told his parents he wanted to leave farming, they told their boy that "such a thing was never heard of" in the DiCosimo family that had been on their land for many generations. When Vince got a bit older, he still helped out on the farm, but he watched, waited, and he dreamed about success in North America. But, he also knew he had to learn English. "I told my mother that I didn't want to go to Canada to be a dummy. I want to know what's going on. It would be to my advantage when I eventually left Italy for Canada." He also realized that if he took the time to learn English that was time he wouldn't have to spend toiling out in the fields.

His older brother, Stanley, was already working in Niagara Falls. Stanley recalled that he wanted to send $50 to their mother so that Vittorio and Dora could learn English and maybe eventually come to Canada. But their father,

Giuseppe, said Stanley's money was best spent on Vince who had already declared that he wanted to leave home.

Vince said his English teacher, Guido la Fortuna – who taught him for about a year – was "broke" most of the time. For this reason, the teacher would sometimes accept a bribe of two cigarettes each class if Guido would just let his pupil, the crafty Vince, leave early to be with his friends.

The teacher scolded Vince. "He said: 'Hey, it's your mother's money, so you should really attend class and get some results.' But I told the teacher I would rather be with my friends."

Even after a year of instruction, Vince admits that his English was "no good. I didn't pay attention."

Vince, the reluctant farm kid, also used to convince his father that he simply had to leave the fields early, telling his dad that he was obligated to study for his English tests. As soon as his dad let him leave work, Vince was off to roam around town with his pals. The English lessons were forgotten.

His mother, knowing the boy wanted to leave Italy, eventually said: "You know, you don't have to go anywhere; you will do well here on the farm." Vince told his mother he wanted to "go on my own, and become rich. I have to find something that I like. I told my Ma that I had to do what I had to do." But mother insisted that he would "never become rich because 'you will have nothing over there to start with'."

"She told me the best I could do was to become a labourer, or work in a factory."

Just after the war, immigration opportunities for Italians were opening up. To places like Argentina, Brazil, Chile, Venezuela, and Canada, among a few others. America seemed tougher to get into. Vince's own father was thinking of going to Chile, but decided against it. His dad had two brothers, Angelo and Vincenzo, in Argentina. So, Vince's father went there in 1949 to try his luck.

"Father left us and said 'Listen, you guys keep doing what you are doing with the farm, I'm going to stay a couple of years and then I'm going to make a decision. Either you come there, or I am coming back'."

When his father went to Argentina, Evita Perón was in power. His father lived with a niece, Filomena DiCosimo. Giuseppe wanted to meet his brother Vincenzo (the other brother, Angelo, had died in 1947.) One day Giuseppe was sitting outside on a veranda and saw a guy go by on the sidewalk. He thought it was Vincenzo, his brother. His niece confirmed for Giuseppe that it was, indeed, his brother, Vincenzo. Giuseppe was shocked that his own brother avoided him.

Vince's dad's brother eventually explained to Giuseppe: "Argentina is like this – business is first, before family!" Vince said his father was so upset about this family slight that he decided to return to Italy after only about two years in that country.

"My father also wasn't too crazy about Argentina, didn't like what he saw and he wanted to be back with his family. He didn't want to bring up his kids there."

On returning from his Argentina adventure, his father gave his sisters some fine fabrics out of his luggage but all Vince got was a piece of lamb skin which his father figured could be made into a pair of shoes for his son.

The result was that the local shoemaker couldn't cut the skin properly for shoes. But he did have enough "to make a pair of sneakers."

Influenced by all of his father's international travel, in war and in peace, Vince decided he just had to leave home when he was old enough. He thought about India, "because I had heard that immigration was opening up in India," but eventually decided on Canada.

The first time Vince ever left his village was at the age of 18. He went to Rome by train for his medical at the Canadian

Embassy to prepare himself for Canada. In Canada the plan was to live with his older brother, Stanley, who'd already been about a year in Niagara Falls. (Stan came over to be with his girlfriend, Nicoletta, who was in Niagara Falls. Stan and Nicoletta eventually married and their wedding dinner, at The Capri restaurant in Niagara Falls, cost about $2 per guest back in the early 1950s.)

"My father wanted to come with me to Rome for the medical, and I said: 'C'mon, dad, I am 18 years old!' Vince went on the train alone and he eventually hooked up there with a friend from another village, Carmen Vetrone, who was in Rome for the same reason. When he returned from Rome his mother was shocked at his appearance. Vince said his mother believed he probably lost 10 pounds in Rome. Vince said it was only a few pounds – from the pressure and excitement and not eating right in the big city.

Anna and Giuseppe DiCosimo on their San Lorenzo farm. Giuseppe, taking a gulp of water on a warm day, loved working in his vineyards. Anna, the business mind on the farm, also made all the wine for the household – and her "Peppino" enjoyed drinking it.

The two men, DiCosimo and Vetrone, eventually came to Canada separately. But when Vince went to work for Hodgson Steel in Niagara Falls, and gained some authority, he hired Vetrone. His friend worked there for a time, and then moved on to Montreal. The two men remain friends to this day. Vince sees Carmen in Florida.

After Vince passed his medical in Rome, his passport was sent and he went to the "one-guy" travel agency in his hometown to pick up his ticket for the "Conte Biancamano." (After its last voyage, part of that ship was cut away and is now a dry land museum in Milan.)

Vince's ship left Naples on July 12, 1955. His brother Stanley in Niagara Falls was his sponsor for one year. He was so excited about a new life "that I didn't even cry." He stood there holding one suitcase "with a bunch of ropes around it." On the Naples dock were his father and mother, his sister, Elena, and his mother's mother, Assunta. His mother cried. "My mother was devastated. My father was sad, but he would never say: 'What are you doing'? The only thing he said was 'make sure you write'."

"My mother asked me why I wasn't crying and I said: 'Ma, I am going to America, why should I be crying'?" Vince admitted he was "happy and sad" at the same time.

"Everybody was waving a handkerchief and crying. I had a funny feeling, too. I realized I was leaving my family. The boat was going. I was sad. I was a bit choked up. Then we went inside, and I said to myself: 'Don't look anymore'!"

On the boat, Vince said the food was good and he experienced a wonderful new taste, orange marmalade. "Omigod! Even today, I love it." Another treat he had for the first time in his 19 years – orange juice. "In Italy, oranges were eaten, not squeezed."

He believes that his mother was secretly hoping that Vince, in making a new life in Canada, would forget about his romance with Ida Garofano. Mothers are like that. But, the night before Vince left Italy he went to Ida's house and announced to her parents that he was going to Canada and: "I am going to write your daughter. I love her and I want to marry her." Vince noted that Ida's mother already knew that.

It was a 12-day passage to Canada aboard the "Conte Biancamano." He had a cabin with his wife's first cousin, Giuseppe DiRubo, 23, who was going to Montreal, a city in which Vince already had cousins living.

Vince disembarked in Halifax on July 24. When he and his new friends from the ship sent him to a local grocery store to buy some food, Vince could only say "bread" in English. So he bought two loaves of plain white bread.

Leaving Italy aboard the Conte Biancamano. The 19-year-old Vince DiCosimo, fourth from left, has a shipboard dinner with other Italian immigrants during their 12-day voyage to Canada. Their ship cast off from Naples on July 12, 1955. "I was the youngest guy in that picture," says Vince. "The food was good. I had orange marmalade for the first time." Ida Garofano's first cousin Giuseppe DiRubo, 23, is to Vince's right. DiRubo, now deceased, settled in Montreal.

"I'll never forget it. When my cousin and everyone else saw me with just that bread, they wanted to kill me." Indeed, to the young Italian men, raised on good home baking, the tasteless white bread was an insult. "We want our money back," they yelled.

They boarded a train in Halifax and headed out to their new lives. The train seemed uncomfortable compared with trains in Italy. There were no facilities to wash up. "My first disappointment was that train. I arrived in Niagara Falls with a dirty face. When I got to Niagara Falls, at the train station, I wanted to turn around," Vince admits. "I said 'what the hell is this'? There was nothing there. Only one railroad. When you got into stations in Italy there are 20 to 40 rail tracks. I thought this is not a station, it's a garage. But I didn't realize that's the way Niagara Falls was. I was very, very disappointed. The Niagara Falls I saw then, was not the big and exciting place that it is today."

Vince was surprised that his brother, Stanley was not at the station. His sister-in-law, Nicoletta, explained that Stan had to work and couldn't be there. "I thought well that's too bad; I'm going back home!"

(It is somewhat ironic that the very Bridge Street train station in Niagara Falls, where the penniless immigrant arrived in 1955, was leased by Vince DiCosimo about 44 years later. The year before the Niagara Hilton was built, the DiCosimo company used both floors of that old station for the Hilton's planning and administrative offices.)

But, back in 1955, unable to speak English, forced to eventually almost beg for a job, Vince had serious second thoughts about starting a new life in Niagara Falls – especially when he had left a prosperous farm in Italy.

But, things got much better, as we shall see.

7

Courtship and Marriage

"It was the most pleasurable time of my life!"

There was a feast in the town of San Lorenzo Maggiore. Vince, 16, and his pals watched three girls walk by.

"Omigod, who is she?" Vince asked someone about 14-year-old Ida Garofano. "How in the hell am I going to meet her? Right away I moved away from my group to look at her. To walk behind. I said 'guys, I've gotta find a way to talk to this girl'."

(Vince DiCosimo declares today that Ida, to whom he has been married for 50 years, "turned out to be the best thing in my life. If I hadn't had my wife I would not have been so lucky with what we've done. We have worked side by side. She's strong. She is a worker.")

He said that back in San Lorenzo Maggiore, that day in 1950, "it was love at first sight." Ida agrees. "I liked him right away. He was a really good looking guy. Lots of hair." To the young girl, the older teenager looked especially great atop his horse riding through town.

When they got a bit older, they talked seriously about eventually moving to Canada.

At first, Ida didn't know if she wanted to leave her hometown but finally she decided: "Where he goes, I go."

But the teenagers kept their little plan to leave Italy a secret from their parents.

The love-stricken teenager quickly found out about Ida's family background and learned that she had an older brother, Tony, who had a reputation of being tough, and respected. Vince knew he'd have to behave himself.

His "next step" – like a teenager anywhere in the world – was to repeatedly stroll by the girl's home to see what happened. "Every night. I hoped that she would come out. I hoped that she would go to the town fountain to get some water. Just walk by. There was no way you could just talk to her. I wanted to just look at her. I looked. She looked. If she looked at me then, I thought, maybe there was a chance."

Vince explained that, in those days, you didn't just go up and talk with somebody you were interested in. Strict rules of courtship, strict family controls on children, made courtship tougher then, than now. (Ida was actually afraid that someone in town would see them talking, and report that social transgression to the families.)

Vince soon sensed, from the looks he was getting, that there was some type of "understanding." But he also knew that it would take quite a while for them to talk with each other. The romantic impasse was solved by a first cousin, Assunta Sanzari, (now 80), who just happened to be married to Ida's uncle, so a meeting was arranged by the cousin. His cousin thought Vince and Ida were "a perfect couple" so Ida was invited to the cousin's home and Vince was there.

"She was sort of shy, but I got the message that I could meet her again. I said to my cousin 'Listen, I've gotta see her again. So I used to go there. My cousin would have never left the two of us alone."

The family homes of Vince and Ida were about a three-minute walk apart. "My house was four floors high with a balcony on the top floor," recalled Vince. "If I sit out there (on the balcony) and I look to the left I can see her balcony.

Ida Garofano, 16, in San Lorenzo, her birthplace. "Omigod, who is SHE?" Vince DiCosimo asked his pals when he first saw Ida strolling through town.

Every Sunday, as soon as I finished dinner, I would go up. I was waiting for Ida to go out onto her balcony so that we could exchange looks. For some reason she'd come out and we would just look at each other. I was so happy. It was the most pleasurable time in my life.

"Then my mother would say: 'What are you doing up in the balcony?' and I replied that I was taking the sun and my mother said: 'You never went up there before'!"

Ida dressed better than any of the girls around. Vince remembers a particular green dress – "Omigod I loved that dress."

For a few years the relationship blossomed but Vince had never met Ida's parents, Rosa and Cosimo. In July 1955, the night before Vince was to leave Italy to seek his fortune in Canada, he figured it was time to visit the Garofano residence.

"I told her 'Listen, I am going to come over to your house and tell your parents that I want to marry you'. They knew I wanted to marry Ida, but that day I made it official. I told her parents I am leaving for Canada and, as soon as I make some money, I am coming back to marry your daughter. Her parents were happy. Ida was happy but, at first, she was a bit nervous when I showed up."

When Vince was in Canada, Ida went to the DiCosimo home and became friends of the family. "That was the girl. The whole family liked her. She and my sister Dora became good friends."

While living in Niagara Falls, at Stanley's house, Vince said he "really missed" Ida and, at first, they wrote regularly and sent pictures. But Vince got busy and didn't write for a while, so his mother sent him a letter to remind him to get writing again to Ida.

Vince explains that keeping in touch from Niagara Falls with Ida, his village sweetheart, was not that difficult and unlike some Italian men in Canada, he had actually met the woman he'd soon marry. In some arranged marriages, the couple never met each other before the wedding, he noted.

Vince said it was taken for granted that when he and Ida got married, it would be in their village and then the couple would return to Niagara Falls to live. (They have lived in the Falls for their entire Canadian life and raised their large family.)

To gently push things along, Vince's mother bought Ida an engagement ring, "on my behalf," and Ida bought Vince a ring.

Half a world away, the two young people were thinking about each other, their families were waiting and watching, and Vince was trying to get established financially in Niagara Falls.

"But I was broke," Vince admits. "I had a 1953 Mercury. It was the most beautiful car in my life. Even today, I don't think my car is as nice as that one, because that Mercury was my first. But when I decided to go to Italy to get married I had to bring some money home, so I sold my car. After I delivered that car, I cried the whole day."

Vince got $400 for his Merc. He sent the money to his mother.

"I said: 'Ma, here's $400. Use it for our wedding, and if there is any left over, you can keep it'."

The intended bridegroom then bought his ticket and went back across the Atlantic on "The Augustus," after having taken the train from Welland, through Buffalo, (the old T.H. & B. Line) and on to New York City where he boarded the ocean liner.

But, before he left Niagara Falls to return to his home village to get married, Vince was asked to go shopping for a wedding dress for Ida. He found a bridal store and he bought the material for Ida's dress. He said he also got a two-inch-thick catalogue of wedding dress patterns.

Vince went to another store in Niagara Falls, on Main Street, and bought himself a spiffy, long-length, white tweed sports jacket and also some snazzy, baggy pants – both pieces of apparel were North American highest style of men's fashions at the time.

"I thought I would look good."

So, he set out on a rough ocean voyage toward Naples and marriage – a journey that took 10 days. "It was so bad that after two days, you couldn't eat anymore. You couldn't even go in the dining room. A friend of mine, who travelled with me, was sick the whole trip. The Azores were not far away, and I wanted to get off and live there (rather than continue). I couldn't take it (seasickness) anymore. It was bad."

The boat arrived in Naples and the gangway was put down. Vince walked down the plank "in my nice pants and beautiful jacket" toward his fiancé, his father and mother, Ida's father, and many others.

"I was like a big shot."

It was raining lightly, Vince recalls, and after he greeted everyone, he lit up a cigarette. But in the commotion, he dropped more than half the smoke on the ground so he grabbed another a lit that up. Vince's mother, Anna, was surprised that her son – who used to bum smokes in the village – didn't pick up the cigarette half.

"Omigod, Vince, you have changed!" said his mother who reminded him what that half cigarette used to be worth to Vince. "You have been ruined."

"I said 'Ma, please, don't embarrass me. Ma, that's nothing, I've got more cigarettes'."

Vince remembers that when the 17 year-old Ida, an experienced seamstress at the time, saw how he was dressed she called him aside. Ida warned that when they all got back to San Lorenzo, because of Vince's outfit, "we've got to sneak

The farm boy from San Lorenzo Maggiore is on Ellis Avenue in the spring of 1956. Vince worked hard as a labourer in the early days in Niagara Falls, but was determined to start his own business.

around the back streets, you know!" Vince was upset because he'd spent a lot of money on the extra-long jacket and considered it "the best."

"It's not for you," Ida said.

And, when they got into the car at the dock, his mother leaned over and announced: "We've gotta stop at the store and buy you a suit. I don't want you to show up dressed like that."

At the time, the style in Italy was "really, really short" jackets, Vince explained.

So Ida took his jacket to her house and measured it up. Ida wanted to trim 10 inches from it. Vince pleaded for only four. She took off four. Then, when Vince wore the shortened jacket and his baggy pants down to the town square, an old friend came over and told him he just had to shorten his pants.

Finally, after viewing what the men in the village were wearing, Vince became convinced. "So, I told my fiancé, please take another four inches off. And then I started dressing like them."

As his clothing was being re-adjusted just before the wedding, Vince ran into another problem – and it involved a simple piece of paper that he did not have. Vince said that before he left Niagara Falls, he was told by relatives in Italy that, before he could marry Ida, he had to produce a certificate from the Roman Catholic church in Niagara Falls proving that he was not married.

"The priest had told my girlfriend that she had better make sure your boyfriend has that certificate."

Vince explains that Father Michetti at St. Anne's in Niagara Falls had promised him the certificate. But when Vince visited the good father on the day before he was to leave for Italy, the day Michetti said the important piece of paper was to be ready, "he wasn't there. I had to leave."

That caused big problems back in Italy because the priest there insisted Vince produce it. Vince wrote to his brother Stanley in Niagara Falls and asked him to contact the priest. As time went by, and there was no certificate, both families were getting nervous.

Finally, Vince and the village priest visited a judge. The judge said that Vince should write to Canada again.

The marriage day was approaching and still no certificate. Ida's mother suggested that perhaps "some oil," a little gift for the judge, might be appropriate.

But Vince was reluctant to do that. Somehow, even without the certificate, and using some other legal means, "called Article 13," according to Vince, the marriage was eventually permitted by the church.

"My mother gave us a beautiful wedding."

It seemed like the whole town showed up for the ceremony joining Vincent and Ida Garofano in holy matrimony at the Church of San Lorenzo Martire on March 19, 1958. The wedding procession began at Ida's home, and drew many townsfolk as it proceeded to the church. "There were about 20 couples, and then all the kids. The whole town was involved. They threw *confetti* (white candies) in front of the groom and the bride as we walked along and these kids would kill themselves to pick up the candies."

Officiating at the wedding mass were Don Angelo Protaro and Don Antonio Iannotti. (The older priest, Don Antonio, insisted on calling Vince "Americano.")

Vince recalls that, on his wedding day, he had already eaten that morning, so the priests weren't going to allow him to take the hold sacraments of bread and wine – the body and blood of Christ. (Vince had told the priest during confession that he'd eaten breakfast.)

"Listen, don't embarrass me!" Vince whispered at the communion rail, but the priest only whispered back to Vince

Here comes the bride, and groom! Vince and Ida on their wedding day, March 19, 1958, in San Lorenzo Martire Church in San Lorenzo. Vince and Ida came to live in Niagara Falls a few months later.

that he'd only go through the motions, "and I am going to go by you and play the part but I am not going to give it to you."

The reception, and even the honeymoon, were spent at the DiCosimo home on Via Forte. About 75 people came to the home for food and drink after the wedding and Vince noted there were the traditional 10-12 courses.

Vince does not recall any band at the wedding but he remembers that four of his buddies woke the couple up at about 2 a.m. with a serenade outside their window. The couple invited them in for a drink.

Like many newlyweds the world over, Vince said that at the time of their wedding, "I was broke." In fact, his mother supplied him with some spending money while he was home for a few months. In the year he and Ida got married, his older sister, Elena, got married, and his wife's brother, Tony, also got married "so we were three newly-wedded couples, and we used to all get together."

After the wedding, Vince took his mother aside. He asked her if the $400 that he had sent her from Canada – the money from the sale of his beloved 1953 Mercury – was enough to pay for the wedding. Vince admits that he was embarrassed when mother explained that the $400 was hardly enough to buy the *confetti*.

The married couple left for Canada from Naples on May 28, 1958, aboard the 1,000-passenger "Saturnia" along with Vince's married cousins, Lorenzo and Antonina Sanzari. These relatives had never consummated their marriage. Vince and Ida surrendered their cabin.

Ida was seasick on the voyage. His cousin's wife also got sick. The voyage took eight days with stops at Palermo, Sicily, and Lisbon, Portugal, and then on to Halifax.

At the stop in Palermo, the newlyweds decided to take a horse and cart for a half day of sightseeing, and Vince thought the driver said the charge would be 1,400 lire and off they went. When they returned, the driver asked for 14,000 lire.

Newlyweds Vince and Ida, married for two months, were in Lisbon, Portugal, in May, 1958, during a stopover on their honeymoon voyage to their new life in Canada.

"I said, 'hey, listen, are you crazy? If I thought it was 14,000 I would have never come with you'! Vince said to him: 'You got no choice; either you accept my 1,400 lire or you can chase me because I am leaving'!"

Then, the two couples fled the scene.

The ship arrived in Halifax and they took the train to Niagara Falls. Vince remembers that he always felt the Canadian trains were not as modern as those in Italy. While travelling earlier by train in the 1950s through Canada, Vince was always amazed at the many forests and wide open spaces, dotted only with isolated farm houses.

The size and the scenery of Canada always impressed him. "Because in Italy there are no forests, it is all cultivated. Either you see grapes, or you see cities. I thought I would end up in a damned forest."

Ida admitted that she was "nervous" about coming to Canada "but I knew that one day it would be okay." Her biggest worry arriving in Niagara Falls was that her new husband didn't have a job and there didn't seem to be many jobs available at the time. (Ida now admits that she could never image that the family would do so well in Niagara Falls and that "one day my kids would be the owners of the Hilton.")

The couple settled at the home of his brother, Stanley, and his wife, Nicoletta, at 5734 Dunn Street with Vince's older sister Maria DiLibero, who died in 2004 at 73, and her husband, Nick DiLibero, now 76, also living in the home at the time. (Vince eventually became a business partner with Nick.)

Vince admits that the young couple "didn't have a penny" to give his brother for room and board.

But Vince says today that he was reticent to accept any dead end and menial job. "I worked hard not to have a job and Ida was concerned about that."

Vince had heard that Burgess Battery was hiring so off he went. He walked to the company and then waited in line with about 100 others at about 7 a.m. By 9 a.m. a big car rolled up and the boss got out walked by everyone. The boss then sent a man out to say there would be no hiring that day. That happened day after day.

"I went to Burgess every day, for 30 days," says Vince. "After 30 days I was the only one standing there." He adds that his strategy at the time was to try to "tire them out" and then they would eventually put him on the payroll.

Vince's job strategy worked. Someone finally came out and told Vince, who was standing there alone, there were no jobs to be had.

"Are you still here? I said 'yes'. So, the man led Vince to the company's zinc department and said he could have a job cutting up some old metal pieces with a machine "but after one month you are gone. Understand?"

Vince began to make about $70 a week, enough to "get by" and to pay his brother. But it was tiring piecework and his leg, which operated the cutter, was always sore after a shift. Hot baths at Stan's home helped relieve the pain.

As soon as they arrived in Niagara Falls, in 1958, Vince and Ida unpacked their wedding clothes and had this photo taken at a Niagara Falls studio.

8

From Digging Ditches to Doing Deals

"I am firing myself!"

When Vince DiCosimo recalls his early days as a labourer in Niagara Falls (the mid to late 1950s) and, later, making his first business deals, he credits family, friends, and the people who loaned him his first investment money for his eventual success.

Then there is the "fear factor," or what seems to be the man's lack of it. As he plunged into debt, or tested any new business, Vince said he was always sure of the possibilities. He had "no fear" about the outcome. He always felt everything would work out. It usually did.

"But every time we bought a piece of property," Vince says with a laugh, "my wife had a good cry because she thought it was too much. But then, after, when things worked out, she was the happiest person alive." Vince said he usually tried to negotiate all real estate deals himself and only in later years did a professional realtor assist him.

"When I look back I think: 'You know what? I am not special. A lot of people smarter than me, more educated than me, they couldn't do what I did.' I only realized this now that it was the people around me that made me special. They believed in me. And I ended up with the right people."

Like his older brother.

Stanley DiCosimo came to Canada and Niagara Falls in 1954, a year before Vince arrived in 1955, and when Vince arrived in Niagara Falls, he said directly to Stanley, "Where's my job?"

At the time, Stanley was working for Smith Brothers Construction of Niagara Falls.

"I was 19," said Vince. "I was skinny. Curly hair. Well dressed. Stanley said to me: 'Take it easy, take it easy, I've got to talk to my boss'. "

Stanley now says that he supported his brother in Niagara Falls when he first arrived and was glad to do so. He knew his brother was ambitious and he knew he would succeed in life, even back then. "He didn't care if he went broke or didn't go broke," said Stanley. "He had no fear. He took chances. And he built a great family."

Even before he worked on a few jobs with his brother, Vince went to work in nearby Welland with an Italian contractor from Niagara Falls, Dominic Senese, and Senese's group of bricklayers, all Italian immigrants. Vince recalls climbing into a truck on a steaming hot July day and arriving at the Welland job site. "I was the fresh one. The bricklayers said: 'Here's the young guy.'

"The temperature must have been 100 degrees. I had to mix the mortar. I had never done that before." Vince admits that when he tried to draw the hoe through the thick mortar, "I went into the tub."

The foreman gave Vince another job. He took the inexperienced labourer to the basement excavation of a house. A truck with cinder blocks arrived and the driver put a plank down and began putting the blocks down on the plank that led into the basement.

"These block were the big ones, 75 pounds each. For the driver, he had been doing it so long they were like feathers to him."

"Mr. D." Una bella vita

It's 1955 in Niagara Falls. Vince is in the laneway outside the Ellis Avenue apartment of his brother Stanley, and sister-in-law, Nicoletta, where he was staying. The Italian immigrant strikes the confident pose of any 19-year-old set on making his mark.

Vince tried his best. He got hot. He stripped down to his underwear, and "I couldn't breathe." The lady next door brought out a jug of lemonade to the young man standing in his underwear.

By 3 p.m. Vince had finished work. No one else was around because they were over at another job site, so Vince left work and tried to walk home alone, back to Niagara Falls. By 5 p.m. the others had finished up, and were on their way back to the Falls. They found Vince on the highway, about five or six miles from Welland.

By that time Vince had reached a firm conclusion about being a bricklayer's helper: "I told them I was going home and I wouldn't go with them anymore. I told them that I didn't come to Canada to kill myself. I told them they left me there with no water. Keep your money, I said. I am going home. That's it, I never went back." Vince retired from the bricklaying trade after that one day in Welland.

And always, in the back of his mind, was the dream of starting his own business. "I didn't come to Canada to work for somebody else anyway. I was always looking for an opening to go on my own. But I still thought my brother Stan would have a job for me. I asked him every day. Finally, he said, 'You know what? My boss said you can come.' So, I came."

But Vince didn't know English, and the boss at Smith Brothers Construction, a guy named Earl, was a bit unsure of the teenager. But he seemed to like Vince, so he took the kid home in his truck, showed him off to his wife, fed him in his own home, and eventually returned him back to work.

Vince's first Niagara Falls job was with his brother at the site of the present day Vincor International, the old Bright's Winery location on Dorchester Road. He was making $1.25 an hour.

"I saw this pile of stone and my brother said we had to spread the stone flat. I said to my brother: 'You're crazy, how are we going to do that?' Oh, he said, it was easy, we'd just get some shovels. I said, 'You know what? I didn't come here to shovel stone! This is not what I wanted in Canada!' But I was young, so I started shovelling."

And, true to Vince DiCosimo's lifelong passion to do everything inmediately, and with vigor, he shovelled too quickly. The Smith Construction boss was concerned that the new employee would collapse.

"The boss thought I worked too hard. I was too fast. That's the way I am, too. Every time I work, I gotta do it fast. I guess the message was that if I keep doing it that fast for the day I would end up in the hospital."

Later, Vince had a talk with his brother and repeated to him that manual labour, or working on a farm, was not his Canadian Dream. (Vince said that his brother Stan suggested, in about 1957, that they buy a small farm property in the St. Davids or Virgil area. "We went to see a farm around Virgil, but I told my brother, Stan, 'You know what? I was born on a farm. I got out of that damned farm because I hated it. If I gotta do farming here, I am going back home.'")

"I also told Stan that I didn't think I left my parents' home to come and do manual labour." Vince explained that in the new land he felt slighted somewhat because, back in Italy, he had come from a family that was running successful farms and here he was making low pay at poor jobs.

But he stayed with Smith Construction for a while – ending up on one occasion at the Norton plant in Chippawa in a trench in the winter digging into the frozen earth. The wind was howling. What was worse, the trench collapsed on him and he had to be dragged out.

"I got out of there and I told my brother I'm not staying with this (ditch digging) and I'm not coming in anymore. My brother got scared because he was responsible for me."

Ida's first winter in Canada. The wool-wrapped youngsters from Italy are dressed up for stepping out in Niagara Falls in 1958. They were now staying at the newly-purchased Dunn Street home of Vince's older brother, Stanley.

Vince explained that he thought it was unfair that he had to walk 30 minutes each day just to get to the Smith construction yard. Only when he arrived did he know whether or not he would be required to work that day.

"They treated me like a slave. I said to my brother: 'You tell those guys that next time they want us to work they can call us the day before.' I eventually quit. My brother wasn't happy."

Jobless again, Vince walked through the city's new subdivisions to see if any building tradesmen needed a helper. He soon found work mixing plaster with Venzon Plaster of Niagara Falls.

"I ended up doing the whole thing. The jobs of three. I was fast. The boss said, 'Hey, you stay with me. I am going to make you a plasterman.' I said, 'Listen, I didn't come here to be a plasterman. I gotta find something better than a plasterman.' "

Vince explained that, at that time, he didn't mind hard work but he simply did not wish to "fall into the trap" of having to rely for the rest of his life on a job he didn't like but could not escape.

So he quit. Again.

Eventually, roaming around Niagara Falls, the jobless, penniless, recent immigrant spotted the Hodgson Steel shop on Bridge Street. The company was a busy ornamental and structural steel concern at a time of a building boom in the Niagara Peninsula.

"I still didn't speak a word of English yet. I spotted this guy that I felt was an Italian boy, and I said, 'Hey, I need a job!' and he said, 'What can you do?' "

At this point Vince offered up a little white lie in order to try to advance himself. It worked, because it got him in the door, but he was soon found out. Vince explained to the Italian-speaking Hodgson employee that he had just left a

"12-man steel shop in Italy" to come to Canada. In reality, "I had never seen a electric drill or a welding machine in my life," he admits.

About this time – with the Hodgson foreman becoming more and more suspicious – the man who gave Vince some real breaks in his early working life, Fred Hodgson, the tall, patient proprietor showed up at the shop. Hodgson ordered that the young immigrant be given a chance.

In the shop was a pile of ornamental railings that needed to be ground up. When he was given the job, Vince continued his impersonation of an experienced metal man by asking: "Where's the file?"

Eyes popped out all around the modern shop but the new employee was nevertheless handed an electric grinder to attempt the job. The machine flew out of the hands of skinny Vince and seemed to "go all over the shop and it never stopped." Vince was asked for an explanation so he stammered, in Italian, that "uh, in Italy the machines are different and they are slower and easier to handle."

But the truth was that the young farm boy from San Lorenzo had never even seen a piece of electrical shop equipment before that day.

The company, and Fred Hodgson, nevertheless stuck with their new man and Vince was soon confronted with a big pile of ornamental railings that needed to be cleaned. Just two hours later, Fred Hodgson himself strolled over and observed, remarkably, that the job was finished.

Vince was in solid at Hodgson Steel.

From that time on, Hodgson took a real shine to his new man, the earnest Italian guy who could just never say 'no' to any assignment. Or, as the company soon found out, admit that he didn't know something.

"Fred Hodgson was from Welland," said Vince. "He was so smart. Omigod, I learned so much from him." Not only was Hodgson smart, he had compassion for someone who showed raw ambition but would be held back because he didn't know English. So Hodgson arranged for Vince to knock off his shop duties at 4 p.m. and take an hour of English language training (with pay) in Hodgson's own office. Hodgson and his wife were the teachers.

"So then I picked up English fast. They liked me."

It is now clearly apparent that they had to like him because the overly confident Vince DiCosimo was a true test to the Hodgson company in the following months. Niagara's successful businessman recalls two particular instances at Hodgson Steel when his own blunders made him step forward and declare: "I'm firing myself!"

One involved a job in nearby Thorold. Fred Hodgson had a contract to provide the structural steel for the new post office on that town's Front Street, and he needed a load of steel trucked over from the Niagara Falls shop.

"Fred said, 'You got a licence?' and I said, 'Yah.' I never wanted to say 'no.' He asked me, 'Do you know where Thorold is?' and I said 'Yah.' But I had never been in Thorold." Vince had also never driven a dump truck. Not even a car.

Vince recalls that as he drove out of the yard he turned onto Victoria Avenue as soon as he could "because I wanted to disappear because I was too close to the shop. I wanted to disappear from the eyes of the people at Hodgson."

Then the road rose on the railway bridge on Victoria. It was then that the truck slowed as Vince tried to figure out how to shift, so he then put his foot on the brake and tried the emergency brake lever. He grabbed another lever and pulled it up. It was the dump handle. He looked into the rearview mirror and saw the truck's box rising.

"Then there was this big noise and I realized that something was wrong. People were blowing their horns at me, so I got out of the truck."

Vince's "Home" Office – The kitchen of his Niagara Falls home in the late 1950s became the young man's home office where he made plans, wrote reams of notes, and studied English from time to time. Vince admits he has always been a heavy duty note maker.

With his entire load of steel spread out on a main thoroughfare of Niagara Falls, the brash young man from San Lorenzo "realized what a great country I had come to. These people behind the truck, they knew that here was this dumb kid. So they helped me load the truck up. It took all day. Then I turned around and went back to the shop. I never went to Thorold. I went in the office and said, in Italian, 'Me? Go home! I am firing myself! I am no good.' "

After his words were translated to Fred Hodgson, the boss responded, "Tell Vince, don't worry about it. He doesn't have to leave. Just tell him the next time when I ask him something and he doesn't know, he's got to tell me he doesn't know."

Soon, when Vince got the idea of how ornamental railings were built and installed, Fred put him in charge of the department. He even had one man under him. Then, Vince was told to load up a truck with ornamental railings for 15 houses in Toronto and ordered Vince to go with another employee and install them.

"I had never really visited Toronto," Vince confesses today. "So, I couldn't find one address; I couldn't find one house."

After about eight hours, he returned to Niagara Falls with all the railings. "I thought I had done so bad that I might as well quit." He explained to his translator, George, "I am sorry but I have caused too many problems here. Tell them that I am quitting. I'm firing myself. But also tell Fred that he owes me $10." So George explained to Fred that Vince was quitting, but he added that Vince wanted $10 from the company for gasoline.

Fred exploded: "You tell that son-of-a-bitch, crooked Vince, that the truck only takes $5."

"Hey, what's the matter with you?" Vince said through his translator, "I had to fill up twice!" Fred seemed dumbfounded but, Vince believes today, he seemed to appreciate Vince's enthusiasm even though he was screwing things up. "You tell Vince he stays here," Fred declared. " 'He is not going nowhere. I need him.' He knew I was not a quitter, that I wanted to be a success."

The two serious firing offences apparently forgiven, Hodgson appointed Vince his driver, designated to picking up his wife in Welland at noon hour in his convertible, taking her shopping from time to time, and also delivering various sets of construction drawings to offices and job sites around the Peninsula.

Vince says that Hodgson's compassion for him, giving him a second and third chance, "taught me lots, and helped form his own tolerant attitude to his many employees today. As Fred demanded of him 50 years ago, Vince expects his employees to be straight with him.

Soon Hodgson Steel, which was paying him only 60 cents an hour, had appointed Vince the hiring agent for the company, screening immigrants with potential for work in the shop. Most were Italian.

"OK, so what did you do in Italy?" Vince asked one. "I was a welder," he answered. "Prove it to me," said the hiring agent. Vince had taken the dark lenses out of the welder's mask and the "welder" fired up "and he was going blind. I was young, you know, and this was fun. He came out of there and he was crying." Vince's cruel hijinks at Hodgson Steel, he admits now, had a few people in the shop "wanting to kill me."

One young man showed up and said he was a welder. "I said, 'Listen, I'm going to hire you on one condition – you've got to teach me to weld.'" Even though Vince learned to weld, and ran a Niagara Falls steel fabrication and structural steel company for many years, he admits that he still longed to become a successful businessman.

And a rich one.

After Hodgson Steel – where he couldn't seem to draw much more than 60 cents an hour – Vince moved on to Niagara Structural Steel in St. Catharines in 1957 where he got a big boost in pay to $2.50 an hour, good money at the time.

In December 1957, Vince returned to Italy to marry his girfriend, Ida Garofano, in their hometown of San Lorenzo Maggiore. The two had been writing to each other. The wedding was in the village church on March 19, 1958. The newlyweds came to Canada and Niagara Falls on May 10, 1958.

When the couple first came to Niagara Falls they stayed at the apartment of Stan and Nicoletta. Through the early years, Stan worked with Vince for short periods of time at his various businesses. But Stan admits he did not have the entrepreneurial spirit of his younger brother and eventually ended up working as a welder at Ohio Brass for 18 years.

Today, Stan, 78, still a vigorous worker, is in charge of the 34 automatic drink dispensing machines at the Hilton Niagara Falls Fallsview.

When Stan thinks about it today, he believes Vince's strong business ambitions had their roots in their mother Anna's drive and good business sense. Stan admits that both he and his brother sometimes spent money foolishly, but they did not learn that trait from their mother.

In 1959, Vince and his brother-in-law Nick DiLibero, husband of Vince's sister, Maria, opened an ornamental steel shop, DiCosimo and DiLibero Ornamental Railings on Bridge Street.

At Vince and Nick's first business, the Niagara Falls fire department stepped in right away. They were concerned about safety, so Vince scattered a bunch of buckets filled with water about the building. This was his firefighting system.

Vince knew he had to "bring the work in" to the new business. He felt the two relatives "had to make it." He decided on creating some pamphlets for advertising. At the time, there was a successful company called Peninsula Ironworks so, Vince admits, "I stole one of their brochures which showed the different kinds of railings. There were beautiful pictures. I went to the printers and told them to change the name to DiCosimo Ironworks. I started to sell. Three months later I got sued." Peninsula was after him for stealing the main art in the brochure. But Vince found out that Peninsula had no copyright or registered trademark on the pamphlet. The DiCosimo/DiLibero company carried on.

A 25-cent shot! Vince and Ida paid their 25 cents and posed for this photo booth portrait near the Rainbow Bridge in Niagara Falls in 1958.

It was touch and go in the beginning. The two men didn't have the money to buy the proper drills to get into the concrete to anchor their ornamental railings. They rented a drill when they needed it. On one of the jobs "we broke the whole damned veranda."

Vince discovered that he was a fairly talented salesman. He visited homes when he knew families were at their dinner hour. At times he'd be selling three or four railing jobs a day. The two business partners even offered customers a time payment plan, but payments weren't always on time. They also hired a salesman who travelled about Ontario and sold railings on the payment plan, but he pocketed the money and disappeared on holiday. Vince decided the company should drop "this far away stuff" and stick to the Niagara area market.

In 1962 Vince left DiCosimo and DiLibero Ornamental Railings and opened DiCosimo Ironworks on Montrose Road. He took in as partners two brothers from St. Catharines and, in 1964, changed the name to Columbus Plate. Soon Vince was meeting a 50-employee payroll. It had been just seven years since he arrived penniless in Canada. "I was getting pretty big." The company engaged in structural steel work and Vince concentrated on selling steel directly to general contractors building small apartment buildings, schools and churches. Vince became dedicated to the business to the point where – after dinner with his family – he would head out to an architect's home where he would stay until midnight learning how to read construction drawings so he could bid more intelligently on various jobs. Learning to read engineering and architectural specifications was "something I wanted to know, to understand my business better," he says.

Vince also became a good welder and was even named a Canadian Welding Bureau inspector.

He was fast off the mark. "I always woke up without an alarm at six o'clock, and on the road by seven." But he'd leave the house only after breakfast with his wife and he always made it home for dinner with his family. "It doesn't matter what business required, I was always home with my wife and kids." Vince hated working nights, and he still does.

"Then I took these two (St. Catharines) partners in and I made a deal with them that I would be out of there within two years because I just couldn't see myself anymore in the steel business. I was looking for different businesses, then I saw this car wash and B.P. (British Petroleum) Co. gasoline station at Victoria Ave. Avenue and Willmott Street St. in Niagara Falls.

Vince went in and improved the car wash by building, with his own hands, a fully automated operation. He ran this until he sold it in 1973.

His young boys, Joe and Frank, were told by their dad to "make sure nobody goes through the car wash without paying, because I was busy washing the cars. I told them two things: 'Make sure you collect the money, and watch you don't give too much change back. And if somebody comes and tells you he's my friend, tell him that you don't know nobody. If it's true that he's my friend, tell him to talk to me at the back. But make sure you collect the money first. Just say, 'If my father knows you he'll give you your money back'."

Vince said some so-called friends also wanted free gas, took it, and then rode off. "In those cases not only did I lose money, but I lost a friend."

While in the car wash/gas business, Vince kept his eye out for any opportunities along River Road, a location that enjoys steady tourist traffic. Vince knew that once visitors have seen the natural wonder of Niagara Falls, the draw is usually to travel downriver to the rapids, whirlpool, Whirlpool Aero Car, and the quaint and historic communities of Queenston and Niagara-on-the-Lake.

"Everybody who comes to Niagara Falls, it doesn't matter where they stayed, you know, Lundy's Lane or wherever, they always had to go by my doors on River Road to see anything. The traffic was there."

By this time, Vince (still running the car wash and still a partner at Columbus Plate) had bought a lovely old brick house at 4027 River Road at Glenview Avenue, and he moved there with his young family. In the successful life of this entrepreneur, this purchase of a sturdy, Victorian-era residence was the key initial move into the tourist trade. A smart move that led to much better things for the hard-working DiCosimo family.

Vince recalls: "I decided to have a little snack bar in 1972 at that house. To fill things out. This is the famous Jumbo Burger Villa. I hired these kids. They opened up. Everything happened from there on. Every year we were getting better and better. The whole family. We were never scared to work."

The veranda of the family home was the snack bar. The family lived upstairs in a spacious and "lovely" apartment. The snack bar had two tables at first, then six. (That house, and the entire eatery, would probably fit into the check-in lobby of the family's present day Hilton Niagara Falls Fallsview.) From that small snack bar, the DiCosimos increased their business interests at a fast pace, and by the year 2000, they had 10 hotels and 11 restaurants.

Ornamental railing business. Steel company. Gas bar. Car wash. Snack bar. Didn't Vince think back then that he was trying too hard, taking on too much?

"No, the idea was to test different things and to see which one I would like and make some money in the future. That's where I would go, with whatever worked. And that's what happened. I had to find what would work for me."

Soon, Vince and Ida began to see that at the modest River Road venture "there was more of a future for us than any-

Vince and the kids. It's 1969. Vince Jr. is on dad's lap at the family's new home on Coach Drive in Niagara Falls. Joe is on the left – then there's Frank and Anita on the right.

thing else I had done. It was better just to stick with it and work at it and keep going and I guess that's what we did."

A local man named Ronnie Smart had wanted $17,000 for the River Road house. "I didn't have a penny." Vince offered $11,000 and Smart agreed. Smart held the mortgage. Vince made the payments from his salaries from the steel company and gas bar/car wash. In the meantime, he had a new home built on Coach Drive where the nicer homes were. They lived there for three years.

But Vince soon realized, as the snack bar business picked up and the couple's time was required there, that they really should be living on River Road so they sold the Coach Drive house and moved back to the upper apartment. The family lived and worked there for about 20 years. (His Days Inn was eventually built on the site.)

With three young children, Ida kept busy in the River Road apartment home. But in the evenings she and Vince would come down into the snack bar to check out the activity. Ida said she didn't mind all the work in those days "because we were so young." She and Vince soon realized that their snack bar might be a winner. "River Road had always been busy with tourists. You know, a lot of people in Niagara Falls don't even know it. They don't know that River Road is such a nice part of the Niagara Parkway.

"I used to go into the cash register and I used to pick up a lot of $20 bills which, in those days, were like $100 bills now. Not too many. So, I said, 'My gosh, you know what? There might be a chance here. We started to see the money and I said to my wife, 'You know what? We've gotta make a decision here, either we are going to keep going with this, or we'll give it up and I'll go get myself a job and we'll live like everybody else.' "

Even though he was still "struggling, struggling" financially at the time, he decided to move out of the car wash and Columbus Plate and concentrate on the possibilities of his tiny hamburger business.

Ida explains that her husband is exactly like his mother, Anna, a sharp businesswoman who ran the farms and expanded them. Vince has a business brain, like his mother, and he is also looking for opportunities and ways to grow businesses. "I am afraid a little bit of taking risks but Vince is not afraid." She admitted that every time Vince told her he had made another big investment, "I'd cry all the time. But I wanted it (investment) too. I hoped it would go through."

Ida said the couple had some "hard times" but Vince would always say, " 'Don't worry about it.' But I worried about it. I worried that we could lose everything." She honestly believed that the banks would take their house and that made Ida "nervous, really nervous."

Today, Ida credits much of the family success to her hard-working children. And she is delighted that today the DiCosimo businesses run as a "democracy" with everyone taking part and having a say. "But they needed their father all of the time."

When he thinks of it now, Vince laughs and confesses that, "My whole life has been struggling, struggling, struggling, omigod, yah. When I opened that snack bar I built everything myself. Chairs. Tables. The first day that we opened we had no signs. Nothing. I made $17. I said to myself, 'If I make more than $17 from that day on I would stick with it.' And I guess we never made less than $17 a day."

Vince tells it like it was. "My wife said, 'I will never work in there.' I didn't like it either; I couldn't even fry an egg. I wouldn't even know how to crack an egg. But that didn't bother me because I always felt that the more you knew how to cook the worse you are off because then you pay attention to cooking instead of running the business."

When Ida realized that the snack bar made only about $80 on the best day, she reminded Vince that she had been making $120 a week (a great wage in those days) sewing at Niagara Rug.

The snack bar food was basic – French-fries, hamburgers, onion rings. Once Ida became more involved in the snack bar, the decision was made to include pizza on the menu. They decided to "go big on pizza" and also offer delivery. "I told my wife that we had better pre-cook some pizzas because I knew that we were going to be blasted (with orders). Thing is, I waited all day and night and, at 11 o'clock at night, one guy calls. I had all these pizzas, pre-cooked, all over my dining room, on the floor, on the table. My kids were going crazy. The delivery guy went and delivered. The next night, one more call. It was the same guy that called the night before. I went to deliver the pizza and, when I got there, the first thing he told me was 'the pizza last night was no good.' I said take this one for free and forget it. I went back home and said to my wife, 'Forget about delivery, no more delivery for us.' "

At the time, customers were ordering just some fries or a coke or a hamburger but, or so it seemed, not all three items at once. "I said, 'We've gotta force them to buy the whole thing. That's when I came out with the Big Meal. I put on the sign: 'Big Meal, Hamburger, Fries and Coke'." This, Vince points out with pride, was long before McDonald's had dreamed of such a marketing ploy.

For his Big Meal he needed big buns so he went to Metro Bakery and they agreed to make Jumbo Burger some oversized buns. Vince is proud that, even today, the bakery still makes Jumbo Buns. It was his idea.

Ida said she worked hard at the snack bar and the kids helped out. She was young, she said, and never complained about the work, but does admit that "one day I cried all day" at the snack bar. The reason was that she made a big mistake. Vince left for work elsewhere and he told Ida that she really shouldn't open up alone but wait for the kids to come home from school. Ida said it looked like there wouldn't be too much business – so she opened up. "In two minutes that snack bar got full," she now says with a laugh.

"I had to cook, and serve, cook, and serve. I started to cry. My kids didn't come home until 3:30 p.m. One of the customers said, 'Don't cry, Ida, I'll come and help you.' "

Ida said today that as the family worked at the River Road snack bar, and Vince worked at other jobs also, she had the feeling "every year, every year," that the DiCosimo family would eventually be blessed with great success.

"The easiest thing would have been to quit," said Vince.

In those days, as Jumbo Burger moved ahead, there was a restaurant a few hundreds yards downriver from the small DiCosimo operation. It was the Whirl Inn Motel and Frontier Steakhouse. The restaurant was always "packed." Vince resented the stiff competition for the River Road tourist traffic. "He was bothering me. I couldn't do anything. He (Whirl Inn owner) felt I was cutting into HIS business so he put a trailer outside to sell hamburgers and hotdogs." His competitor also planted evergreen trees that seemed to hide the view that the motoring public might have had of the DiCosimo business. "He was blocking me out. But the trees were not enough, then he put a fence about 12 feet high. So, you could not see my place until it was time to turn and then it was too late. I was very upset. So, I said, 'That's it!' "

About this time, Ida's mother, Rosa Paolella, died in Italy. The couple returned for the funeral. On the return trip to Canada, Vince began reflecting on his business and he decided that he just couldn't tolerate the competition. "I told my wife, 'You know, what I gotta do is buy the competition out.' She said, 'You haven't got a penny,' and I told her, "You know what, that's OK. Somehow I gotta find it.' "

But there was one problem – the competing River Road restaurant was not for sale.

In the meantime, Ronnie Smart had sold Vince's mortgage held on the River Road property. Vince then travelled to St. Catharines to meet the new mortgage holder, Sidney Orvitz of Income Trust.

"Mr. D." Una bella vita

A riverside picnic with mom and dad. Vince and Ida took Vince's parents, Anna and Giuseppe for a drive along the Niagara River Parkway during their three-month visit to the Falls in 1970.

127

"We connected right away. He was really nice to me. We became good buddies." It was Orvitz who eventually helped Vince buy out the River Road competition. (They remain good friends to this day. And in later years, Vince would rely on Orvitz to help out from time to time. "When there was a little (financial) hole to be plugged, Sid was always there.")

Vince figured that Fred Hardy, the wealthy owner of Frontier Steakhouse and Whirl Inn Motel, would never sell it to him so he had to devise a scheme to make the purchase. He called a friend he had in real estate, Herb Cowan, of Canada Trust. Cowan informed Vince that the owner would never sell to him.

"I said we are not going to tell him it's me. 'Tell him you've got a guy from Toronto who wants to pay him big money.' " In a few days, Cowan had the place listed for $250,000 – big money at the time. Vince then wanted to know whether or not if he paid the full price for the property could the man refuse the offer. Cowan said no.

"I called Sid Orvitz and said, 'Sid, I got to make an offer here, can you help me?' "

Orvitz couldn't handle it himself so he went to two partners. Sid and the two potential moneylenders made a visit to the DiCosimo apartment and "peeked over" to see the subject property, and "they liked it."

It was 1979. Vince soon had a signed offer for $250,000 cash and when Fred Hardy – now bound by the offer – found out that DiCosimo was the new owner, he went ballistic. "I told my kids to go and take down that fence. They got their friends and they took crowbars. They began smashing the fence." But a neighbour, who didn't know that Vince now owned the property, and the fence, called over and warned Vince that "those kids are going to end up in jail."

Vince ended up leasing, at $15,000 a year, the newly purchased Frontier Steakhouse to his teenage children, Joe and Frank, who worked there when not in school.

"Mr. D." Una bella vita

Anna and Giuseppe DiCosimo in the kitchen of the family's Via Forte home in San Lorenzo in about 1980. "Peppino" loved his pipe and mugs of his wife's good wine.

The children had begun helping out at the Jumbo Burger Villa, which was renamed Mother's Pizzeria in 1975 and La Doria in 1977. Vince now also had another 11 rooms to rent in the Whirl Inn motel, so the family's commercial activity along the river was gaining force. (Soon the DiCosimo's single Niagara hotel, the expanded Hilton Niagara Falls Fallsview, will have about 1,000 rooms to offer.)

"My businesses were now being run by my family," said Vince. "I kept everybody busy. The best part was that as long as you don't worry about the hours you put in it was okay. If you started putting things on paper, you would never do it." In those days everyone chipped in, in every way, to improve the family's situation. The kids worked the cash, Ida often cooked, Vince took orders. The boys also went down to the Falls at Table Rock House and passed out cards to sightseeing bus passengers promoting the Jumbo Burger Villa – a soliciting activity that was strictly forbidden by the Niagara Parks authorities.

Vince had put the boys up to it.

"They were small. I said, 'Listen, when everybody comes out don't give the driver a chance to come off of the bus, you jump right in. Tell them (passengers) that your mother is the cook at the restaurant and you want them to come and eat with us."

The parks police soon showed up.

"They called me up and said, 'Vince, listen, your boys were soliciting business. They are jumping on the buses.' I said, 'Whatya mean, where? I don't know nothing! Listen, I cannot stop my kids.' " The parks cops warned Vince that if their own father didn't stop them, the lads would end up in jail.

"I said, 'You know what, why don't you do me a favour? Keep them inside for the summer, they are bothering me.' "

"The guy says, 'You don't mean that, do you?' And I said 'Yes'."

"But you gotta advertise, and my boys were doing that," Vince explains. "If you can't afford to advertise, you can't afford to be in business." The boys did lure some buses to Jumbo Burger that summer – before the cops arrived.

The Tam O'Shanter Motel on River Road was old and had 17 cabins, one of the earliest motels in the city. Vince bought it for $64,000 in 1974. There was a house with the property, which had two apartments.

"It was good for us. It was a good start. There was no hot water. A guy called and asked where was the hot water. I said, 'Don't worry, the hot water comes from far away, but it will get there.' The guys says, 'It's been over an hour,' and I said, 'You gotta wait a little longer.' "

Vince explains that there was an incredible demand for his $20 rooms. The rooms had seen better times. One large-sized guy fell through the floor and complained. Vince scolded the guy for breaking his floor.

"I remember one Labour Day, not only did we charge $150 for the cabins, but we had some extra mattresses in the garage and my sons put them on the lawn and they rented the mattresses. Honest. That is not a lie. That's when I started thinking that this hotel business might be okay. For some reason I always saw this getting better every day. And I saw the kids growing up in the business. And I said maybe this is for us."

At the time, Ida had been working as a sewer at Niagara Rug in downtown Niagara Falls, but she eventually quit that job to spend more time raising their family and working at the snack bar.

But Ida was good at Niagara Rug, where she worked for about 10 years. The owner there pleaded with her to come back in to repair some rugs from time to time. Stan's wife, Nicoletta, and about "40 other Italian ladies" also toiled at the rug company.

Vince returns home. He was about 34 years old, working hard at his new businesses in Niagara Falls, with four young children to support, when he returned to visit mom and dad in San Lorenzo.

"Ida did well. She's a worker. She never complained."

The first River Road ventures put the DiCosimos on the path toward eventual ownership of motels, hotels and restaurants throughout Niagara Falls, just before they sold these assets to raise the money for the 58-storey addition, now under construction, at the Hilton Niagara Falls Fallsview.

Besides Sid Orvitz, there was another financial backer who helped Vince advance his businesses. His name was Charlie Best, and he was with the Canadian Imperial Bank of Commerce. Best cautioned Vince, in about 1990, about using U.S. financial backers when Vince was about to purchase the Niagara Hotel in Niagara Falls, N.Y. Vince didn't listen at first, but Best proved to be right, "and we closed the (hotel) deal with the CIBC."

The DiCosimos were on their way. The pace of business picked up – and so did the risks and the rewards.

9

Building the Family Business

"I was called the King of the Franchisers."

The Tam O'Shanter Motel, on Ferguson Street near River Road, was one of the oldest motels in the Honeymoon Capital of the World. Vince bought the 17-cabin complex for $64,000 in 1974. There was a house with the property which had two apartments.

Already owning and operating the Jumbo Burger Villa on River Road, the Tam O'Shanter (a round Scottish cap with a bobble in the centre) was Vince's first venture into the guest accommodation business. (By the time the 520-room Hilton Niagara Falls Fallsview was completed and officially opened on May 19, 2000, Vince and his family had owned and operated four international franchises businesses.

Through those years, because he had the "master franchise" for Days Inn in Niagara Falls and also held franchises for Best Western, Denny's restaurants, Comfort Inn and Hampton Inn, Vince became known to some people as the "King of Franchisers" in Niagara Falls. All of these business operations were owned and managed by six separate companies.

In 1990, Vince bought the 200-room Niagara Hotel in Niagara Falls, N.Y. and renamed it "Days Inn." The hotel had been built in the early 1930s. Vince and his son, Joe, both admit that in the early 1990s the family company had become over-extended, they had been moving "too fast" into the hospitality industry and they got into a financial bind. But the DiCosimos stayed the course, got some financial advice, did a restructuring and steadily moved solidly back into the black. His friends and family all say that Vince's unshakable optimism was the key to his success. Ida has noted that Vince was always of the view that if everything fell apart, "we'll start again."

But the family company held together and the DiCosimos moved forward to their biggest success story, the construction of the magnificent, 36-storey, 520-room Hilton Niagara Falls Fallsview. The family already owned and operated the 15-storey Days Inn on Buchanan Avenue, and this had also been run as a Hilton and then amalgamated into the new building.

Over the last few years, to attain the funds to begin construction of the new, 58-storey wing of the Hilton, Vince sold his many hotel and restaurant properties to be able to raise the $200 million needed for the wing, highest building in Niagara.

Today's magnificent Hilton had its genesis in the 17 creaky cabins of the Tam O'Shanter. True to Vince's life-long driving ambition, he realized that if one old motel could ring the cash register, a few more motels and hotels, would make an even louder sound. Vince prided himself with not ever having to pay top price for any of his acquisitions. "I always wanted properties that were down here (Vince indicates with his hand a lower price level). And, I wanted properties that I had room to improve. I didn't wanted to pay for what someone else had done, I wanted only to pay for what I wanted to do to the property."

"Mr. D." Una bella vita

A quarter century of love, happiness, hard work. It had been 25 years since the teenagers, Vince and Ida, exchanged wedding vows in the Church of San Lorenzo Martire. About 150 guests, family, and friends gathered on March 19, 1983 in Niagara Falls for a 25th wedding anniversary celebration at "The Love Boat" restaurant on Victoria Avenue. Vince and Ida, their four children and 11 grandchildren, are now planning to celebrate the 50th wedding anniversary. From the left, in this 1983 photo at the DiCosimo's Cardinal Avenue home, are Frank, Joe, Vince Jr., Vince Sr., Ida, and Anita.

137

Vince said he was never scared of buying any place when the owner said: "I don't do that well." To Vince, that was his main challenge, to improve the look of the building, and its operation. "That's how you create your assets."

By 1980, the various DiCosimo enterprises were providing a steady income for the DiCosimo family of six. Frank and Joe, were young men taking more and more responsibility in running the businesses and the teenagers Anita and Vince Jr. were also employed.

After the Tam O' Shanter, Vince bought the 11-unit Whirl Inn and Frontier Restaurant on River Road. Then he bought the 30-unit Rapids Motel. This was rebuilt and converted to, at first, an Econolodge and then a 96-room Days Inn. With this, La Doria restaurant was operated.

Then, in 1980, he bought the 30-unit Shady Rest Motel, beside the Whirl Inn, on River Road. Soon, the Shady Rest and the Whirl Inn were converted to a 66-room Comfort Inn, operated along with the Frontier Restaurant.

Along the way, he bought the Rapids Hotel (not to be confused with the motel) also on River Road, demolished this structure and then built a 96-room Best Western motel.

Also along River Road he bought a Howard Johnsons and converted it to a 110-room Hampton Inn.

In about 1988, Vince bought the Lundy's Lane Motor Inn. Lundy's Lane, in the historic heart of Niagara Falls, is one of the city's busiest thoroughfares of hotels, motels and restaurants. The motor inn was converted to a 125-room Days Inn. Vince and the family also owned and operated a Dairy Queen ice cream franchise there, one of the oldest such outlets in Canada. Their miniature golf course was also a big success. A 175-seat Denny's Restaurant was soon built and operated by the DiCosimos in the same Lundy's Lane complex.

In 1989, Vince bought, for about $15 million, a 15-storey hotel that was under construction on Buchanan Avenue at

Murray Hill. (It was the beginning of the incredible building boom in the area, just uphill from lush Victoria Park and the famous falls.) That incomplete hotel was purchased from the Menechella family and converted into a 200-room Days Inn by the DiCosimos. Then, just behind his Days Inn, at Stanley and Murray Hill, Vince purchased the Liberty Inn from the Zappitelli family. He converted this motel into a 110-room Days Inn, and built a Denny's restaurant at the corner of Buchanan and Murray Hill. (This had to be demolished for the new Hilton wing, and the Days Inn has to be levelled to make room for an 800-vehicle parking facility to service the expanded Hilton complex.)

At the time that Vince owned nine hotels and motels and 10 restaurants, it really goes without saying, that the family company was in a great position to offer Americans, and those visitors from the Hamilton and Toronto markets, very attractive "Niagara Falls packages." Vince said that his print advertising budget alone in the large circulation *Toronto Sun* newspaper ran to about $1 million a year.

Vince DiCosimo was always, and still is, a hands-on type of guy who enjoys being involved in the day-to-day activities of his many businesses. An accomplished handyman himself, and always full of ideas about how to improve any building, Vince said that when he bought another motel or hotel, "my job was to go in and check it out and make sure everything was working. I was more like a maintenance man in those days. I went in to see the changes I had to make. If I didn't like the lobby or the counters, I'd say 'Listen, we've gotta fix this up'." We called people in to help us re-do it. But I used to also do a lot of maintenance work by myself, plumbing, electrical. I just loved to do it."

As his room count increased, at about the time he was operating four motels/hotels, Vince got the idea that the company had to establish a "central registration" centre.

Vince was worried at that time that his best people to meet and great his guests always seemed to be tied up in some back room answering the phone. They then hired more people for the lobby. "I said you have to separate those two jobs (phone reservations and greeting guests at the front desk). Vince said he did not think any of his potential guests should be "put on hold" on the telephone, while an employee welcomed other guests at the desk.

Vince and his son, Vince Jr., then the marketing manager as he is now, set up a central reservations office and it worked well. "The advantage of that was that we never lost a customer. If someone calls for a Days Inn on River Road and they couldn't afford the price, we could send them to Lundy's Lane. It worked. It paid off."

Vince does not mind being classified as a "trouble shooter" in those busy days. "I used to sneak into the reservation room. I'd stay behind, and listen to the way the girls answered the phone." If he saw a courtesy problem he wouldn't say anything to embarrass the employee but pass it on to the hotel manager.

"I loved to do that and I didn't do that because I wanted to bother them (employees). I wanted to make sure that my system, my business was being run properly by everybody."

Vince would also check out his kitchens and he'd be aghast at seeing "trays of fries" just sitting there, already cooked, but not being served. They were preparing too much at one time. "I wanted portion control." The days of Vince motoring around Niagara Falls checking on every room and kitchen dwindled down when the DiCosimo hospitality conglomerate expanded. "My kids said, 'hey, pa, you gotta stop'." His children were worried that their dad was being worn down with the "little things." His son Vince confided that all of his children, his own business partners say to him, "we don't look at the French fries, we look at the 'over all,' how much money we make at the end of the year. You cannot count every fry, pa."

But Vince laughed, and told his son that "if you do it my way, you'll make even more at the end of the year. But I was smart enough to realize that I don't have to fight my kids. They're not stupid. But, you know, at the end of the day, they were doing it too (counting fries). They said 'Dad, go play golf, we'll run the business'."

Vince said he eventually eased up a bit but he gave his kids some business advice: "Meet with your managers every day. And you crucify them at the (board) table," he said with a laugh. "Even if they give you good figures, you tell them it's no damned good. You tell them it is not enough. Don't believe their (managers') numbers, they have got to back them up."

But Vince said he was also always eager to praise his employees who did well. "The ones who were no good, I didn't give a shit, I'd tell them off."

Through the years, because Vince has made so many good friends in Niagara Falls he has these friends call him to ask for jobs for their children. He usually just passes these names on to his managers. If they screw up, even if they are children of friends, they're gone, said Vince.

Vince adheres to his company's hiring process, through written applications, and he knows he cannot discriminate. On occasion, Vince explains with a wide grin, a little "X" used to show up, mysteriously, right beside the name of an Italian kid. 'When it's time to hire, look at this kid,' I would tell them.

"My kids would laugh and say: 'Pa, you can't do that'!"

"Hey, are they trying to tell me how to run my business? I pick whoever I want," said the man who was once a young Italian kid looking for work in Niagara Falls.

10

Getting High With Hilton

"Omigod, I was filled every night!"

The one deal that probably began to change things for the DiCosimos – that eventually resulted in the construction of the $60-million, 520-room Hilton Niagara Falls Fallsview was the deal at the corner of Murray and Buchanan back in 1994.

Victor and Cosmo Menechella, who now own the Marriott Hotel, were building a 15-storey Quality Inn there. Vince and his children played golf with these two gentlemen and "we are still good friends." The men wanted a certain price for the incomplete hotel. Vince said he didn't have that kind of money but he consulted with his children.

The "good deal" was eventually signed for $13 million but as soon as the transaction was done, work stopped on the hotel. "There was a lot of work still to be done."

John Broderick, the lawyer for the Menechella's, bet $100,000 that the DiCosimos would never close the deal.

The hotel opened as Days Inn and "Omigod I was filled every night," Vince says today. Nearby hotelkeepers wanted Vince to boost his room prices but Vince explain that he was carrying a large mortgage and he couldn't. "The way to pay the mortgage was to fill up every night. We used to have 200 walk-ins every night."

Vince, a franchise operator for Days, admits that he occasionally had his differences with the head office, and it was usually because he went his own way and didn't always adhere to the fine print in the contracts.

Vince has a laugh about his talk with a Days Inn proprietor down in Florida who asked Vince if, when he signs the franchise agreements, "do you read all the small print?"

"No!" was Vince's answer.

"Dammit! That's why you own six Days Inns and I've only got one," the guy said.

The Days Inn by the Falls prospered, but the DiCosimos all knew that "we wanted to build, to expand," said Vince.

"So, Joe (his son) made some calls, some inquires about the Hilton" Vince explained. "The Marriott was done, the Sheraton was already here, so the only other high end chain was the Hilton."

But the Hilton officials initially contacted didn't think it was possible to convert a Days Inn to a Hilton. A represenative of the Hilton chain visited with the family back in the late 1990s. "Hilton is not Days Inn," he said, and urged the DiCosimos to "prove" that they could be a Hilton. "This is the big league," he stressed.

The Hilton representative who initially visited "couldn't make the call" of allowing the DiCosimos to open a Hilton, so the company's North American franchise president, Jim Abramson, of Beverly Hills, eventually made a visit to Niagara Falls and Vince took Abramson out to "wine and dine" at the city's landmark Skylon Tower. Vince, Joe, Frank and Vince Jr. were there with the president and two other Hilton officials. The president "liked wine," Vince noted. "We connected right away."

Joe and Frank DiCosimo had meanwhile teamed up to "convert" one of the Days Inn rooms into a Hilton-style accommodation."Frank said leave it with me. He went to Toronto, picked up some furniture, marble tops…"

After dinner and much wine, Vince took the Hilton president to see the Days Inn suite that Frank had "Hiltonized."

The president approved. "These guys deserve the Hilton chain," he said. "We all looked at each other and said 'can we really do this'?"

The city demanded "a nice looking building," and that was the intention of the DiCosimos. "We didn't want just another square box building." On Abramson's recommendation the family contacted architect Howard Field in California. (Stan Downey, of Toronto, was a main architect on the new Hilton.) Vince figured he wanted "a lot of arches" in the new hotel, just like buildings in his hometown of San Lorenzo. "Every church and every house."

So Stan drafted a plan that showed a hotel with a lot of arches. That plan was shown to Field who turned to his wife, Jane, and asked for her opinion. "That reminds me of the monastery I was in for about 15 years," said Jane Field who trained to become a nun. Howard Field thought the rendering looked "like Fort Knox."

Soon, Field, who became a good friend, took a piece of paper and a magic marker, "and he drew the hotel, just the way you see it now."

But there were problems. Vince wanted the new Hilton to be 36 storeys, but there was a Niagara Falls bylaw against that. Vince and his family lobbied for permission to go to 36 storeys. He said he was even threatened by one individual, "a big operator in Toronto," who claimed that Vince was paying off city councillors to vote in favour of allowing 36-floors of construction. Vince admits that he telephoned various councillors and asked them to side with his 36-storey plans.

The six DiCosimo "kids" at the grand opening of the Hilton Niagara Falls Fallsview on May 19, 2000. From left, are sisters, Dora, Maria, and Elena. In back are "the boys," Vittorio, Stanley, and Vince.

The matter went before city council and there was such a controversy that the height issue was probably destined to be settled by a lengthy (and costly) session of the Ontario Municipal Board (OMB). The family didn't want this because it would delay the project. Vince gives a lot of credit to Toronto lawyer, Steve Diamond, an expert on the OMB, for helping him fight the opposition and get his hotel.

Vince said that "at the end of the day city council couldn't stop me." Council eventually approved the construction of the 34-storey Hilton Niagara Falls Fallsview which opened on May 19, 2000.

"To us it is just another hotel.We have got to dig another hole and pour more concrete. And we have to go up there close it off and open the door and get people in it and that's it. Do we comply with the Hilton standards? We exceed and surpass them."

The opening of the Hilton in 2000, and the great potential in that falls view location for expansion, convinced the DiCosimo family to sell off its other assets for the money to build the 58-storey Hilton wing.

"I made a decision to get out of River Road when we first opened the Hilton. I told my kids we have got to centralize, we have got to run one big property; so that the whole family energy goes to one building. It's so much easier and also the results are so much better."

The single greatest business accomplishment in the career of Vince DiCosimo, and of the others in the family business, will be the opening of the new, $200-million, 58-storey addition to the Hilton Niagara Falls Fallsview in the spring of 2009.

"The end product," Vince declares, "is going to be the best in Niagara Falls. When this thing is done, and open, there will never, never be another hotel project like that. They can never tell me I've got too many rooms, they are my rooms! We never worry about putting people in our rooms. We can almost see them in there already."

Vince admits that some of his friends feel that his plan to offer more than 1,000 first class Hilton rooms, is too ambitious. "They say 'are you crazy? Why do you need that for? You already got too much!" Vince answers that if everyone had such small ambitions, and didn't believe in progress, "we would all still be living in caves. I tell them that life is a gamble anyways. I always say that I am not a gambler, but (in a way) I am one of the biggest gamblers because I gamble everything I own (on new projects like the Hilton expansion.)

11

Vince's Children and Spouses Discuss Dad

"He just sets examples."

Vince said all four of his children are humble people, hard workers and not showoffs.

"They never tell you: 'Who the hell are you? Look what (possessions) I've got here!"

As partners in the hotel business, Vince depends on them, is proud of them, respects them as individuals, and admires their strong work ethic. They all say their work ethic came from their hard-working parents. The whole family strived in the early years and – to the many business associates who know the DiCosimos – the "payback," in the form of financial success for all who contributed, is being experienced now.

Vince said one example of how well the family works together occurred last summer. The family, Ida, Vince and the four children, met together to discuss their most ambitious business project, the $200-million wing.

He said everybody was open and frank with each other while discussing the project and wanted to know the thoughts and feelings of everybody else. "It was such a nice meeting," said Vince. Ida wanted to talk to the kids and tell them how she felt. She did. I didn't have to say much because I had been talking to them all the time." Ida admits that she feels the hotel will be too large; but she's been worried about her husband's ambitious projects before.

"Mr. D" said he could not be prouder of his children. "I treat all my children the same, but I know how to talk to them in four different ways. I can ask the same question, in a different way, to the four of them."

"They love to come to work in the morning," said Vince. "They love what they do. If they have to come here 24 hours a day it's never a problem. It's not just one of them. It's all of them."

Vince thinks it was important that he and Ida always insisted on having all of their evening meals with their children and discussing the day's events. He knows his own children now do that with their own children and Vince said that daily gathering is important to the unity of any family. "You have to just sit down, have your dinner together and talk."

Vince also admitted that he hated, through the years, to bother his children by asking them for help. "I always thought that my kids were doing something else, they were too busy, even when they were young."

Joe DiCosimo, 47, is the first born. He deals with most of the key financial matters of the family hotel business. He also believes he is a "visionary," like his father, looking always at the big picture, new projects, and always well into the future. "I can see the future. I can see what's needed. I pushed my mom and dad to come up here and buy this hotel when I could see things moving."

"Me, and my brothers and my sister are products of him and my mum," Joe stated.

Joe said his father was never a taskmaster as the kids were growing up. The children never felt forced to work for the family – but they did anyway because they wanted to.

"Dad is at the age where he is content now," said Joe. "The kids have pretty well taken over the business. My dad is semi-retired but he is involved every day. He will always be involved. He is 71 years old and as sharp as a whip. He is enjoying life. He's making friends; he could make friends with the Eskimos one day and the next day he could go and talk with the prime minister of Canada."

Joe admits, "I pushed a lot. I was very ambitious myself. I probably got it from him. At a young age, I was the type of guy, like him, to trade security for opportunity."

He said his father backed him with encouragement on whatever he wanted to do. "He never said 'no'. He just set examples. He worked hard. My mum worked hard."

Joe recalls that when he was about 12 years old, while working at his dad's car wash Morrison Street, his dad asked him to sit on the side of River Road, where the family was living, and count the cars. It was part of his father's "marketing study" to see if there was enough traffic to warrant opening up the snack bar there. There was, and that modest snack bar was the family's initiation into the Niagara Falls hospitality business.

Joe thinks his father was a "little different" from the average immigrant who came to Niagara Falls for a better life. His father educated himself in the language by going to school and starting businesses that would allow him to work for himself.

"If he wanted to end up working for somebody in a factory he could have stayed back home and worked for his dad on the farm," Joe observed. He does not think it was necessarily "all about money" with his dad – he simply wished to be his own boss. "He wasn't in it for the money."

Joe is asked what made his father successful?

"A couple of things: He had the mentality that he was going to give up security for opportunity. He didn't mind making a little less to seek opportunities. And he had a hardworking wife, my mother, and some kids who were willing to work and not stray off and go the wrong way."

Joe said it was never a matter of mother and father forcing the kids to work. "It might be the other way around. We might have pushed them more. It was weird, being the oldest I always wanted to be in business; I never wanted to go to the beach."

He said it was never "about paycheques," as the family was building their businesses. He does not believe that's the main consideration today.

Joe uses a phrase that is often used by his father: "We made things happen; we didn't wait for things to happen."

The eldest son, the "money man" in the family business, admitted that there were some financial setbacks in the early 1990s, probably due to becoming overextended in businesses that were "growing too fast."

"That's partly my fault," he admitted. "We were growing fast and my dad never said 'wait' and never said 'no'. It wasn't about that. He could have gone broke, but if his family was intact and everybody was happy, that's what counted."

One problem back then, Joe explained, was that they were building a hotel down on River Road and the trust company that was backing them went bankrupt. "We had to finish off the hotel without the backing of the finance company. We got overextended. It was sort of a self-induced (financial) restructuring, a planned restructuring. We learned a lot from that."

Vince is asked to talk about his son, whom he calls "Joey."

"Since he was a little boy, Joey has always been smart," said Vince. "He's bright. He never gave me problems. Never. We never had a fight. Sometimes we didn't agree; even now we don't always agree, but you know what? That's okay.

At the end of the day we always make the right decisions. Joe is a leader. He's sort of like me. I was just like him when I was his age. He wants to get things done. His way. But we talk about it. Whatever decision is made together it is always the right decision. Joey is very creative too. He explores ideas; he talks to different people. He's got all good qualities. Always talks to his brothers and sister."

Vince admits that Joe can get upset with government officials who can impede progress. On occasion, father has had to try to rein his boy in. One time, Vince recalls, his son snapped at a local civic official, stating: "When you build your own hotel, you can do whatever you want! My hotel I will build the way I want it!"

Vince said his son is open to his ideas and is willing to change his opinion on business matters. Joe always takes on a lot of responsibility, said his father. He added that he is proud that Joe has been so involved in local charity golf events. He noted that his son is a good golfer and usually gives his Pa about eight to 10 strokes. "Joe was also a good soccer player and basketball player." He said Frank and Joe, only a year apart, played soccer together. "They didn't play hockey. I don't know why. I guess they couldn't get up early in the morning. I didn't like that myself."
He said Joe, who worked from an early age in the family hotel and restaurant businesses, went to Brock University for three years in the hospitality program. But he told his father "the teacher tells me I know more than him."

Two serious incidents in Joe's life stand out for his father: once Joe was knocked out in a soccer game and another time he was knocked out when a bundle of insulation was blown off the roof on a windy day during the building of the Hilton. It struck Joe. "He almost died," said Vince. "It knocked him onto a pile of pipes. He was unconscious. They had to rush him to the hospital. Frankie was with him. There were four or five guys there but Joe was the only one who got hurt." It took Joe a few months to recover and in the meantime, Frank, handled his brother's duties, "he had to take over and finish the hotel."

At the soccer game, Joe, who was about 15 years old, was punched while in a fight, and had to be taken to hospital. "They called us and we had to run over to the hospital."

Frank DiCosimo was born only 14 months after Joe. Growing up, the two brothers were close. They played together, worked together, fought together.

Today, Frank, 46, is vice-president of operations for the Hilton, the day-to-day, hands-on guy.

Like his year-older brother he learned business as a kid, "taking cash" at Jumbo Burger Villa when he was about 10 years old. "I have no regrets," said Frank. "We had to do it. Even if we did get paid we used to give it all back. We enjoyed it."

Frank attended Niagara College for "my chef papers" but he got "so tied up" with the family business, he never graduated. He doesn't regret that, he said.

Frank said he has enjoyed working with his father. "He is great. He is incredible. Everyone loves him. He is so easy to like. We respect him. At the end of the day, he makes the calls."

He said he believes that the DiCosimos have been successful in business "because we communicate. At the end of the day we all have our roles. We could probably do each other's duties if needed. Joe's in charge of financing, Vincie is in charge of marketing. They could come in and do 'operations' anytime. I could probably do marketing. But we all have our defined roles. And we just communicate. I think that is the key. We are close."

Frank believes that his father's success is based soundly on "vision," and the entrepreneurial spirit. "My father was not cut out for an eight-hour day, 40-hour week job in some factory. I mean he's been there and he's done that. But he's always looked beyond that. He always had the vision. And he always had the gift of be able to talk to people. My dad could have been a politician."

Frank stresses that his mother was a strong influence on the success of her husband. "If my mother wasn't my mother, my dad wouldn't have had anything, I don't think. She's a strong women, and behind him 100 per cent."

Frank's dad is supremely proud of the job Frank did to convert one of their Days Inn rooms to a luxury suite of Hilton's high standards. It was done so that the family could impress the California-based company and land a Hilton franchise for Niagara Falls.

Frank said Joe made "the pitch" to the Hilton corporation, but Frank and his crew converted the demonstration suite so that the Hilton president could decide. It took Frank's crew three days to convert a Days to a Hilton. "We took down walls, put in a tub, king sized bed, wallpaper, rugs. We started from scratch." They landed the franchise.

If Vince has always been proud of Frank, the son says the feeling is mutual: "I hope I turn out half as good as he is. Half as good and I would be happy. And my kids love their nonno. He is a loveable man."

Frank said that one of his "favourite times" with his father was when he and Joe, their brother-in-law Giancarlo, Giancarlo's brother, Joe, his uncle Stanley, and his dad went back to Italy to see his grandfather, Giuseppe. They were in San Lorenzo for about two weeks, "and it was the best time," said Frank. "Omigod, we ate and drank, went out to the vineyards, visited my uncles. My uncle, Vittorio, just loved us being there. We brought my grandfather some Crown Royal. My grandfather had the shakes then; but once he put his hand against a glass of wine, he stopped shaking. My dad brought us around to all his friends. Everyone loves my dad when he goes there."

Vince talks about his son, Frank:

"Everybody likes Frankie. He is one of the nicest guys. People get friendly with Frank. But if you do something bad to him... Omigod. He remembers, and he won't make peace with you anymore... That is the way he is."

He said Frank is key, the point man, in the day-to-day operation of the Hilton. "Anybody who wants to do anything, they go to Frank. Not only that, but if the managers have any problems with an employee, they go to Frank. And then he guides them; Frank wants to get involved in everything."

Vince enjoys playing golf with his family and he confides that Joe used to be the best golfer. He thinks Frank is better now. (Sorry, Joe) "Vincie used to be the best when he was about 17. Right now, Frankie is the good golfer. A lot of times he says he wants to score 80, and then that is just what he does. He is serious about it. Frankie comes to play golf and to concentrate. He will never hit a second ball. He gets very upset if he misses a short putt early in the round that it screws him up the whole day."

Vince said Frank was "a little rougher" than Joe while the two boys were growing up. "Frankie is very stubborn. Even today." When the kids went to Mount Carmel school "I had to go there every week when they would call me about Frank." Grandpa enjoys pointing this startling fact out to Frank and Barbara's children.

Vince recalls that Frank used to have a lot of allergies, as do others in the family, including him.When Frank played with his friends, rolling around in dirt and grass, the boy used to come home "all swelled up."

"I used to say: 'Frankie, you can't do that anymore, you gotta watch yourself. There are a lot of people in my family with allergies."

Growing up, Frank and Joe "were like twins," said their pa. They worked together and played together. "And my kids never gave me one ounce of problems. You know what I am saying?"

Vince pointed out that Frank is a good cook. After the family took over some restaurants on River Road, Ida DiCosimo taught Frank how to cook breakfasts. "Boy, this kid could cooked a thousand breakfasts at a time. He was so fast. Boom. Boom. Boom. He was amazing. He also used to help my wife make pizza."

Anita DiCosimo, 43, is a smart, vivacious business-woman who is in charge, along with her brother Frank, with the day-to-day operations of the business, including personnel matters. Anita is also the social organizer of the family, speechmaker, and the strategist who so successfully masterminded the wildly successful, surprise 70th birthday party for her father aboard a cruise ship in Florida on March 13, 2006.

She's daddy's darling, his only daughter, "and my dad will do anything for me. He is so generous, and so caring and just loves his kids and grandchildren. He will do anything for any of us. He will just go out of his way to please us. He wants to make sure that everybody is the same and equal." She is greatly appreciative of his and her mother's roles in teaching her and her brothers the way of business and the way of life. Both of her parents were people who did not hold themselves up as the final authority on everything. "I could say 'no, pa, you are wrong.' He allowed that. That, I think, was so important." She noted that her parents were not people "that you had to agree with no matter what."

She describes her father as a kind and gentle man who expected much of his children – but gave them freedom, encouragement, and listened to them. "He could get the ball rolling – and then we were on our own."

"He wasn't too strict at all," she said. "He was a good father. He never really got mad at us. He's easy going. We grew up in the business, so I just respected his way of bringing us up. If he said be home at 11, I was the type of kid that I would be home at 10."

Anita said all the children worked in the various family businesses. She started at age 12. "As soon as we came home from school we had to put on our uniforms and get to work." Anita's first job was clearing restaurant tables. "I wanted to work. It was just a way of life for us. My father used to say to me: 'Okay, you watch how the waitresses work, and then maybe, in a couple of weeks, you can pick up' (clear tables)."

One bonus of working as children was that many of their friends also worked in the DiCosimo businesses. "We always had our friends around us and at the end of the night we'd have pizza together. It was exciting. We were contributing but we never got paid when we were young. But anything we wanted, we always got."

Indeed. When Anita was only 16, she was given a new Honda Civic by her father.

Anita said she believes the secret of her father's great success is the fact that he is a "people person. He always told us that, in business, you have got to have good people skills. He is not afraid to speak to anybody. He doesn't feel inferior to anyone. He can make friends with anybody. The friends just attach to him. He'll do anything for anybody, but don't (cross him.) But, then again, even if you hurt him he still doesn't treat you badly, doesn't hold a grudge." She added that, besides his warm personality, her dad is also no one's fool when it comes to the cut and thrust of business, the dollars and cents. "He knows. He is really, really smart in math.

"And, my father was not scared to take chances. Even when he came from Italy, with that language barrier. If he failed, he failed. He picked up the pieces. He is fearless. But he is very sensitive. He is a Pisces, you can tell. And, as he gets older, he's more sensitive."

Anita said that she is happy her parents are enjoying a good retirement. "They deserve it. They both worked hard."

Vince talks about his Anita: "Anita is very close to me and my wife. She was born here in Niagara Falls but she has been going to Italy a lot because she married Giancarlo who is from San Lorenzo. When she goes there people tell me later that I don't even realize how good my daughter is. They say to me: 'You don't even understand how well she treats us, how good she is.' They say to me that there are many people who go there, who are born in America and Canada, who don't even want to bother with us (people in San Lorenzo.)

"Anita can speak fluent Italian," said Vince. His daughter became so proficient in the language because "she cares. Anita thought that my wife will never be able to speak English perfectly, so the only way Anita will be able to communicate perfectly with her mother was to learn Italian. So, she did."

He said his daughter is a social person and a good organizer, "so my daughter, honestly, keeps the family together. The way she does it is that she gets along with all of them. We are lucky that we have Anita."

Vince said his daughter is smart, alert, and sensitive. He also revealed that she relies on him and her brothers to protect her interests in the company. She considers that her brothers are smart and "she trusts them."

Vincent DiCosimo Jr., 37, is the youngest of the children. His responsibilities at the Hilton are marketing and sales.

"What I like about my dad is that he is such a simple guy," said Vince. "He is not showy; he is not show offy. He doesn't have to drive a big expensive car; he doesn't have to have people know what he owns. He wins people over because he is just so genuine. I don't think my father has ever turned anybody 'off' in his entire life. He's different; he's special."

Vince said his father – who wanted this book written not

because of any inflated ego, but for a record for his family – is deserving of a book "because he is just a special person."

Vince believes that his father's great success in business must be the result of his dad being "honest and true, and he is not trying to pull a fast one" with people. "I think he has gotten ahead because of his personality."

In addition to that, his son knows that his dad is a fearless investor and is always willing to take chances, try new projects. "He is fearless to this day." Vince adds that his mother is also a major factor in his dad's success. "My mom is the strongest woman I know. There is nobody who works as hard as my mom. Absolutely."

His youngest son praises his dad's encouragement of his children. "He has never once come up to us and said: 'Kids, I think you are making a mistake'. He has always supported us in everything we have done. He will only give you his input."

His father was not strict with "the kids" growing up. "He and my mother did a great job, because none of us were rebellious, we were all pretty good kids. We all worked in the businesses. I can remember renting rooms when I was 12 years old. We used to have little cabins on River Road (Tam O'Shanter Motel). I used to work the desk every single day."

If he has any criticism, Vince believes that his father, who is "still the big boss", can sometimes become distracted with "the little things" in their hotel business. "Little things DO bother him. There is no doubt. He has always done everything himself. He's looking at these little things. But, it's a good thing. He's still looking."

However, his father is also a craftsman at cutting through details, taking a refreshing overview, and seeing the big picture. "He's not worried about how much money we made because he figures, if we are busy, the money will be there at the end of the day. But he has put enough faith in us kids to run the business. We all do our thing. I do get a call from him

The DiCosimos on the wedding day of Vince DiCosimo and Joy Hessell on Sept. 10, 1994. Vince and Ida are with their children in Victoria Park in Niagara Falls. From left are Frank, Anita, Vince, Ida, Vince Jr, and Joe.

(from Florida) every other day and he will ask me questions. What I like best about him is that he always wants to know what's going on."

Vince noted that his father's warm personality and incredible people skills does not mean that he cannot be tough and pragmatic when it's time to move forward and take action. "He is the only guy that I know who can actually fire you from your job and make you feel good as you are walking out the door," said Vince.

Vince pointed out that his dad is "very handy" with his hands and tools. "He can do just about anything. Hang a picture, paint a wall, fix a car. If I have got a problem at my house, I will call him and he will come and help me fix it."

He said that his family is the most important thing in his father's life. "We are a very close-knit family. We spend a lot of time together. We get along very, very well. Our kids are all very close. I think that is a credit to my mom and dad. My dad cares about the grandkids. He calls them all the time. He wants to know how the kids did in their sports the day before. It's important stuff."

Vince talks about his son, Vincie, "the baby."

"You, know it's funny, because I always treat Vincie like my baby," said Vince. "I remember a couple of years ago, I told Vince I wanted to take him out for dinner, and he said: "Pa. I am 30 years old. Why don't I take you out? But I try not to treat him special by any means. He is a good kid, and has always been a good kid. He grew up without any problems. Like all our kids."

Vince went to Mohawk College (four years in business) and his dad recalls that his training in the family restaurants usually landed him the chore of cooking for his housemates at college. "Being in the restaurant business, he learned how to cook a bit."

Vince's older brother, Joe, met and married Nicole Hessell; and Vince Jr. met Nicole's sister, Joy, when he was about 16 and they eventually married. "All I know is that Joy was working for me as a bus girl, or something (she was about 14 at the time) and I didn't even know who she was," said her father-in-law.

Vince said that Vince Jr.is called "the revenue guy" in the family business. He said his job was always to attract as many guests to the hotels and restaurants as possible. Vince also sets rates. "Me, Anita, Frankie, and Joe, we don't even know the rates of the hotel."

When they married into the family, Vince's son-in-law, and three daughters-in-law got to know and love the strong, soft man who shares his life with them and their children.

Nicole DiCosimo is Joe's wife. She says her father-in-law is a compassionate man who knows almost instinctively when one of his family is having a rough time and he is always there to offer his help. He is also fond of handing out cute or quirky gifts, like weird lights around swimming pools, or bird feeders, and the family loves it. Her father-in-law is addicted to the shopping channel, she laughs, and the family gets a kick out of the merchandise he can accumulate in any one week.

"But I have always had great respect for him, I was a little bit shy with him at first," she said. "He has always been friendly and welcoming. He's a straight shooter. Everyone loves him. We had a nickname for him we called him Smurf." Nicole admits that coming from an English and Anglican Church background she was not certain she'd fit in with an Italian family, but she did. "They were very welcoming." She even converted to Roman Catholicism.

She worked for the family businesses in the early years and she's now in the Hilton accounting department.

Her father-in-law is a wonderful man to all his family and especially loving and attentive to his grandchildren. And they all know it. "He loves to talk about his grandkids, what they are doing. He calls up on the phone, he wants to see what is going on. The grandkids have all been drawn to their Nonno. It's funny, you can put a lot of family in a room and they are all drawn to Nonno. They always go right to him."

Nicole is happy that Vince and Ida enjoy Florida, and she believes they can relax there. She thinks Vince can forget business problems there and just golf and garden and go shopping at the Home Depot every day.

Her father-in-law makes friends "so easily" that "it's amazing." She said he has a "gift" in personal relationship and she believes it is because people realize, right off, that Vince is "a good person."

Son-in-law, Giancarlo Filippelli, husband of Anita:

"When I met my father-in-law I was given an opportunity to face a new life, it was an introduction to the business world. Most of the successful entrepreneurs do not want you to know what they know or have learned, but 'Mr. D.' is different. He loves to share his knowledge with anyone that wants to learn. Most of the time he will tell you that: One of the definitions of leadership is vision and the ability to solve problems. Also the most important thing is your family, their well-being, their future, and to make sure you always have a happy attitude toward life. This way your kids will always grow up with the idea of conducting a successful life. I would like to thank him for this life lesson, because I live by it."

Daughter-in-law, Joy DiCosimo, the wife of Vince Jr.:

"I have known my father-in-law for 25 years. I first met him when I was 10 and my impression of him was that of a generous man who allowed me into his home even though I was not a part of his immediate family. I started working for my future father-in-law when I was 14 and soon after started dating my future husband. As an employer, my father-in-law expected and received respect from his employees. He is a very fair and considerate man. As a father-in-law, he is wonderful. He is always available to listen when my children or I want to talk.

"He is extremely dedicated to his family and grandchildren. My son is named after him and I wouldn't have it any other way. He is the type of man that I hope my children aspire to be. He is the epitome of hard work and determination. He is a role model to his children and grandchildren. My father-in-law has a magnetic personality, which is the reason why he has so many friends and why so many people want to be in his company. I have nothing the least critical to say about my father-in-law other than this happy little observation: Dad's overwhelming affection he feels for our son, Vincent, is something the other grandchildren notice."

Barbara, 46, wife of Frank, talks about her father-in-law:

"He loves people, and is very interested in people," she said.

Barbara pointed out that Vince has "funny ways about him" that are difficult to explain. "I can't describe them. He is comical in some of his ways." She added that she and her mother-in-law "get in trouble" when they laugh at Vince. "She sees the same things I see, or I see the same things she sees. It brings tears to our eyes. We have tears running down out cheeks. We've been told off a few times." She explained that there are just "little things" that her father-in-law does, such as placing a rubber band around his wallet (as her husband Frank is now doing) or using paper place mats for note pads that gets her laughing at her father-in-law.

Barbara said that despite these foibles, she loves and respects her father-in-law.

"He is one of the best people I know. One of the most special people I know. One of my favourite people. He is just so passionate about everything he does. He'd do anything for his family. He's a hard worker. It's nice to see that his hard work has paid off. And he is very proud of his parentage, where he came from and what he has accomplished."

Barbara explained that her mother, May, now 79, worked as a cook for Vince at the Frontier restaurant about 30 years ago. She and her parents came from Manchester, England, when Barbara was young and her parents eventually ran a variety store on River Road.

Vince is great with all of his grandchildren, said Barbara. "We are lucky because the kids had a chance to know their nonno. My father passed away three months before I got married and my kids never had that opportunity to know him. My father-in-law is such a good influence on them."

Ida holds two-month-old son, Joe, at 4370 Morrison St., Niagara Falls. The home, on the corner of Ontario Ave., was purchased for $8,000. After living with relatives and renting their own apartments, it was the first home the young couple owned.

12

At Home With the DiCosimos

"It was the smallest house in town."

Years from now, Vince and Ida's grandchildren, and great-grandchildren, might look around Niagara Falls for the various DiCosimo homes of the early years, the days "of struggle" for "Nonno" and "Nonna."

Some of these homes are gone; some remain.

After a life of hard work, Vince and Ida now live in a beautiful home at 3391 Matthews Drive. The home is situated in a development of larger homes off Mount Carmel in the city's northwest. At this home, complete with an in-ground pool, the DiCosimos entertain their large family and many friends.

Visitors to the home have remarked to Vince that his backyard, a professionally-landscaped little Eden of flowers, trees, shrubs, statues, and bird feeders, is really a little "piece of paradise."

Living beside them are their daughter, Anita, and her husband, Giancarlo, and their children, Marisa and Samantha.

Vince and Ida's second residence, where they live for six months a year, from October to April, is another luxury home in Palm Beach Gardens, Florida, a development called Ballenisles, an upscale community with three championship golf courses. Their home, at 105 Emerald Key in a gated community, has a patio and pool and is beside a system of inland waterways in the West Palm Beach area.

When Vince first came to Niagara Falls, in July, 1955, he stayed at the home of his brother, Stanley, and his wife, Nicoletta, at 4045 Ellis Street. Then, when Vince and Ida came over after they were married in 1958 they went to live with Stanley and Nicoletta and Vince's sister, Maria.

In about 1959, Vince and Ida rented their first apartment in Niagara Falls. It was a second-floor dwelling at 4617 Ryerson Crescent, in a quiet residential area just off Victoria Avenue, a few blocks north of the city's famous Rainbow Bridge. They lived there for about a year.

The DiCosimos soon bought their first home at 4370 Morrison Street – "the smallest house in town." The purchase price was $8,000. It was a good location, said Vince, because he was closer to his welding company on nearby Bridge Street. There were also some other Italian families in the general neighbourhood.(He and his brother-in-law, Nick DiLibero, now 78, opened an ornamental railing shop on Bridge Street.)

In those days, Vince and Ida's social life was centred on visiting other couple's homes. They did not take vacations, and they rarely went out "on the town." These were days of "struggle."

Soon, while he was operating and renovating his Morrison Street gas station and car wash, Vince bought a property at 4027 River Road, overlooking the mighty Niagara River, just downstream from the famous Falls. It was a grand, 100-year-old brick home, of about 2,000 square feet, and Vince had the upstairs renovated into a "beautiful apartment" where the family lived. He converted the downstairs into the Jumbo Burger Villa and began his

Vince attends to the shrubs at their Morrison St. home. He called it "the smallest house in Niagara Falls," but there were many neighbours nearby who were also Italian immigrants and their home was also close to Vince's welding shop on Bridge Street.

scheme of attracting tourists who were motoring by along
River Road.

When business got rolling, Vince and Ida had a new home
built at 5 Coach Drive, in an upscale section of the city. They
lived there for a few years but sold it and moved back to
the apartment at 4027 River Rd. when they needed the
money for their growing businesses. The old brick home
on River Road was eventually moved to the back of the lot
to make room for the 96-room Days Inn was built and the
house was eventually demolished to make room for a hotel
parking lot. All told, the DiCosimos lived at their River Road
home for about 15 years.

As Vince became more successful and his family grew,
he had a large home built at 3515 Cardinal Drive near his
present home. They lived there for 16 years before moving
to Matthews Drive.

At all of his homes, Vince has always enjoyed being the
handyman. Ida is a model housekeeper and good cook.
Children and grandchildren are always there and they, and
others who drop in, are always treated like royalty. Vince is
always making his delicious *espresso*, or pulling out a bottle
of wine from a cabinet, and Ida seems to be always placing
a platter of her wonderful baking on the table within easy
reach.

Little Joe DiCosimo takes a walk on Bridge Street in Niagara Falls, outside the family business, DiCosimo Ironworks, in about 1962.

13

"Mr. D." Gives Back

"Vincenzo, I need those stain glass windows."

There were two standing ovations for Vince DiCosimo as he received the award for "business excellence and humanitarianism."It was presented on Saturday, Nov. 5, 2005, at a formal gala at the Americana Hotel in Niagara Falls – only a few kilometers from the spot where the penniless Italian immigrant Vince, and his brother, Stanley, first picked up shovels in 1955 as labourers.

Then, on June 4, 2007, Vince was given the Silver Palm award from the mayor of his hometown of San Lorenzo Maggiore.

"The whole town was there, and I didn't expect that," said Vince. He said he was deeply honoured to be the first recipient of the award, given by the municipality to any native son or daughter who has had success, made a mark in the world, and contributed to society. Vince received the honour while he and his wife Ida, and daughter, Anita, were on a vacation in Italy. The presentation, made on a stage in the town's piazza, coincided with an annual feast day. Many of the family's relatives were present.

When he handed the Silver Palm to Vince, the mayor, Dr. Angelo Fasulo, said Vince had made his town proud of what one of its people can accomplish.

The silver palm was selected for the award, Vince learned, because the martyr, Saint Lorenzo, after whom the town of 1,800 people is named, is often portrayed with a palm in his hand.

(San Lorenzo was a Roman martyr who was executed in 258. His life is celebrated by a feast day on August 10. He was one of seven deacons in Rome during the papacy of Sixtus II. When the Pope was executed during the persecution of Christians, the authorities asked Lawrence to surrender the churches' treasures to the state. He responded by distributing the money to the poor, for which he was condemned to death. His fearless behavior at his execution was responsible for many conversions. According to one legend, he was roasted to death on a gridiron, and said to his torturers: "I am cooked on that side; turn me over, and eat.")

To honour Vince for his business and humanitarian accomplishments, during the Nov. 5, 2005 gathering in Niagara Falls were Hollywood movie star, Gianni Russo ("Carlo Rizzi" in the Godfather, and featured in other recent movies) and also "Baby Joe" Mesi, the heavyweight boxing contender from Buffalo, N.Y.

The award was presented by the 300-member Canadian Business and Professional Association of Niagara Inc. (CIBPA) The master of ceremonies for the evening, John Palumbo, told the black tie and evening gowned audience that everyone in the association was proud of Vince.

And Vince said he was proud to receive it. "It makes you feel like you've done something right." Expertise in business, and the willingness to give back to his community, "go together for me," said Vince. "To be honest with you, if I had $1 million at my disposal, I would give it away to the right people."

In introducing Vincenzo DiCosimo to the CIBPA audience in Niagara Falls, his friend, Frank DiPalma, said that Vince has done a "tremendous job in the community of Niagara Falls and we are very, very happy that we are giving this award to him."

SILVER PALM AWARD – Vince and Ida were deeply honoured on June 4, 2007 when Vince was presented with the "Silver Palm Award" by the municipality of San Lorenzo Maggiore, Italy.

He is the first recipient of the award. It recognizes native sons who have gone abroad and done well. Vince (left) is shown in the civic centre with, from the left, a local priest, Don Pino, the mayor, Dr. Angelo Fasulo, and Ida.

In his speech, Vince said he was accepting the CIBPA award "for my wife, my children, my family. If it wasn't for them this would never would have happened, I want to thank the CIPBA board of directors who chose me for this." He added thanks to everyone in the room for such a "beautiful night" in his life – every member of CIBPA.

In a video, prepared by CIBPA, and played on a giant screen during the special evening, Vince told the audience that – probably like all Italian immigrants to Niagara Falls – he arrived with only a suitcase and with some high hopes that there would be opportunities available in his adopted land.

He wanted to learn a trade, he said, "because I didn't want to be a labourer… and I was fortunate to become a welder." After he did, he began welding ornamental railings for homes. Then, he went into structural steel in a Niagara Falls business that he ran for 12 years.

How, Vince was asked by the CIBPA interviewer, did a "steel man" get into the hotel/hospitality business?

Vince explained that even while he was working with steel, he had bought a house on Niagara's River Road "and I thought it was the perfect spot to open a snack bar."

The video was especially powerful because, while Vince was talking about arriving penniless in Canada, some of the film footage was of the magnificent Hilton Fallsview Niagara Falls – which Vince and his family erected (with present plans for a 58-storey wing.)

Vince said that his entire family worked well together through the years in developing his businesses.

"Without the family I couldn't do it. A lot of credit goes to them."

Also receiving a 2006 award from CIBPA that night was communiy activist and charity fundraiser, Gino Giallonardo, 76, who won The President's Award.

The guests at the occasion learned that Vince DiCosimo, and his family, had given much back to the community.

The audience learned that well known Niagara wine entrepreneur, Donald Ziraldo, approached Vince and asked him to contribute to Niagara College. The DiCosimo family then donated $500,000 to the culinary school at the Niagara-on-the-Lake campus. The facility is part of the School of Hospitality and Tourism.

"When I saw the facilities and talked with my family, we thought it was a good thing to do," "Mr. D" told his CIBPA audience. "My special reason was that I have 11 grandchildren and some day they might go to that college."

On the video Vince said that he believes that doing well in business and supporting one's community go hand in hand. "We get along with the community. We try to do everything right for the community."

In closing, Vince called CIBPA a group of "wonderful people."

Through the years, the DiCosimo family has donated more than $300,000 to the Greater Niagara General Hospital.

Another example of the DiCosimo love and generosity concerned the late Marilyn Robinson, of Grand Island, an excellent employee, and "a nice, nice lady," who was the hotel sales director for many years. Robinson died of cancer in 2004, and the DiCosimos were there for her husband, John, and their family at all times.

Vince explained that Robinson, sales director and a dynamic achiever, was the key to attracting business to the DiCosimo hotels. Vince asked her why she left a good job to come and work for them. "I love you guys; I love this family," is how she explained it. "She was so happy to see us (businesses) grow. I said Marilyn, listen, be patient, we are going to give you a nice hotel here (the Hilton)."

Vince said that Marilyn only wanted to know when they would open so that she could start selling rooms.

The elegant, boldly beautiful 58-storey, $200-million wing to the DiCosimo's original, 34-storey Hilton Niagara Falls facility – shown in an architect's drawing here – is under construction and set to open in April, 2009. The DiCosimos sold many of their hotels and restaurants in Niagara Falls to finance their spectacular hotel, one of the tallest and grandest in Canada.

Robinson travelled the world selling rooms for the DiCosimo hotels and she was proud to see the companies grow. She was so concerned with the satisfaction of the guests that she would pitch in on some evenings and help out in the kitchens.

"We became such good friends," he said. "She loved my wife, my kids. I felt so bad when she became ill."

Vince kept her on the payroll throughout her illness. She died in her early 60s. "She never told me she had cancer, my kids told me."

"You do things because you want to do them," said Vince. "Not because people then have to do something for you. Inside you feel better. It makes you feel that you have done something right. That's all that counts. What people do for you is not an issue."

Through the years the family has held a number of Hilton Pro-Am golf tournaments to raise some generous donations to the GNGH, where all of the DiCosimo children and grandchildren were born.

The family has also contributed to the ALS foundation. One of their dear friends, Danny Gentilcore, died this year of the disease.

Vince frequently returns to Italy and he does not forget about the needs of the people in his place of birth. About 25 years ago there was an earthquake in Italy and it damaged many houses and churches. The largest church in San Lorenzo Maggiore was damaged so badly that the structure had to be barricaded. The DiCosimo family initially gave $10,000 to this church, San Lorenzo Martire, and the priest asked him for some more money for new stain glass windows. (After the earthquake plain glass windows had been put in to replace the broken ones.)

Vince laughs when he recounts the persistent priest who confronted him and said "Vince, I need those stain windows." The priest even reminded Ida, while she was in

Danny Gentilcore (left) and Attilio Salvatore (right) present trophies to their golfing buddy, Vince, at the Niagara Parks Commission course in 2001. Danny, a great friend of the DiCosimo family, died of ALS, Lou Gehrig's Disease.

the confessional box, that she should push Vince into helping the church again with the windows.

Ida revealed that the priest, who died recently, didn't even seem too intent on hearing her confession. He was more interested in convincing her to prod Vince into helping out.

"I donated $15,000," said Vince. "They had their stain glass windows. They are nice windows."

Vince pointed out to that priest that the church also needs its interior painted. The business-like priest died recently, and a new, younger priest is at the church – and the interior of the church, San Lorenzo Martire, still needs painting.

In the spring of 2006, Vince revealed that he had met informally with about 20 other people and discussed the building of a "Senior Italian" retirement home somewhere in the Niagara Peninsula, probably Niagara Falls. It would be a non-profit, self-sustaining venture that would attract about 100 retired people from the Italian community, but possibly others also.

"If we are lucky we are gonna get old," the 71-year-old explained.

These days, more and more people live longer and "more and more families can't take care of their old folks at home," he said.

Vince said that the organizing group might each chip in $50,000 to $100,000 of their own money, draft a sound business plan, buy some land, and move forward from there. "Then you get the politicians involved. If you show them a good business plan even the bank will help you."

14

The Good Life in Florida

"I'm the poorest guy in the community!"

In the future, if they remain in good health, Vince and Ida plan to spend more time at their beautiful home in Palm Beach Gardens, Florida.

"If we ever get sick, then we are staying with our kids back home," said Vince. "But if we are lucky enough to be healthy, then eventually, every year, we are going to stay a little longer in Florida."

The DiCosimos usually head south in October, return to Niagara Falls for Christmas and the New Year holiday season, fly back down to Florida and stay until the end of March or early April. Their three sons and daughter, their 11 grandchildren, and some in-laws, fly down and visit them from time to time. Vince and Ida enjoy entertaining their family in Florida; some family members stay at the home others stay in a local hotel. Sons Joseph, Frank, Vince, and daughter Anita, and members of their families, are also golfers, so family foursomes are enjoyed. While in Florida, with its Saks, Macy's and other retail outlets not available in Canada, his children and grandchildren enjoy the shopping.

Vince will fly back up to Canada on occasion to tend to hotel business and he is in almost daily telephone contact from Florida with his children, his business partners, back in snowy Niagara Falls. Running the Hilton Niagara Falls Fallsview is a family affair and his children say dad is still "the boss," even while in Florida.

Vince's brother, Vittorio, from his home town in Italy and his sister, Dora, from Milano, and their spouses, flew to Florida to be with Vince and Ida, and the entire DiCosimo family, for Vince's 70th birthday celebration on March 13, 2006. It was a grand occasion, described elsewhere in this biography,

The DiCosimos were attracted to Florida about 20 years ago when Ida visited a relative there for about a week. Then Vince came down to join her, drove around the state, "and I liked everything I saw. We liked the West Palm Beach area. We liked the sun. Then, my kids started looking for a condominium on the phone; there was no Internet then."

At first, they bought a condominium in Palm Beach Gardens, which they had for six years. Then they bought a home on Edward Road in Palm Beach Gardens where they escaped winter for about seven years. In 1999, they bought their present home at 105 Emerald Key Lane, in the Ballenisles community of Palm Beach Gardens in West Palm Beach. It is two storeys with three bedrooms and has an in-ground pool in what Vince calls a "high end" area of town. However, he complains, only in jest, that there are so many extremely rich people around him, in way more expensive homes, that they live "in the ghetto."

"I always say I'm the poorest guy in the community," Vince said with a laugh. "If you found out how really rich some people are here, you would shit your pants. There are some wealthy, wealthy people here." Vince hangs out with a few of them. Some are billionaires.

Palm Beach Gardens is perfect for the DiCosimo family because Vince and Ida, and other family members, all enjoy the many championship golf courses. Vince took the game up when his children bought him clubs about 15 years ago. "I got hooked, like everybody else." He first played at St. Davids near Niagara Falls and eventually had a membership at Lookout Point Golf Club in Pelham, Ont.

He took Ida out for her first round about 10 years ago and now they play together. Ida's in a women's league. Vince didn't think Ida would enjoy the sport because she's "an old-fashioned lady" and she seemed to think, "the ball is too small; I can't hit it." But Ida soon started hitting the ball and, in a little while, got "hooked" like her husband.

There are three professional courses at Ballenisle and the DiCosimo couple prefer the "South Course." Vince said they meet great people playing his favourite game on Florida and Niagara Falls courses. The couple enjoys the company of interesting people from all over the world. "I make friends every day. For me it's easy. I play golf with a lot of people and I enjoy every one of them. I'm not a big sports fan. Just golf."

He recently had the great pleasure of meeting a couple on a driving range. They were from Milano. "They've got a few bucks and they usually rent a house here and play golf every day." Vince enjoyed talking to them in Italian and discovered that they had just bought a house in a neighbouring community and were planning on staying six months a year.

Ida used to enjoy Florida's splendid beaches; Vince said he never did but preferred to drive around sight seeing or playing golf. "When I play golf I hook up with anybody, and I'm not afraid that the guy is a better golfer than me. It doesn't bother me. There are so many people here that you never get bored."

He drives over to the nearby course in his own golf cart and enjoys "four or five hours of fun" on as many days as he can. He bets during each game, varying amounts – depending which pals he is with. He'll even bet with his grandchildren.

One day, as Vince, sitting in his back lawn in Florida, talked by telephone on a blustery cold April day in Niagara, he said it was about 80 degrees already in the early morning "and as I am talking to you, I am looking at the green on No. 7 and the fairway on No. 8. It's beautiful." In the background, workers could be heard with power trimmers, shaping the lush hedges at the DiCosimo home.

In Palm Beach Gardens, Vince helped form *Amici d' Italia* (Friends of Italy) a 200-member social group that began by having pot luck dinners at members' homes. Now the club members sit down to lavish "feasts" (complete with a band) at various banquet halls. On these occasions Vince, and his pal, Lou Alemina from Brooklyn, have been known to sing some old Italian favourites. "Me and Lou, my friend from New York, got up and sang that first time, so since then we've got to sing every time we have party. We get the crowd going."

Dues are only $25 a year. Big dinners with bands are held. "Sometimes it costs you $50 a person." As many as 250 people now attend the functions.

Most of the *Amici d' Italia* members are second and third generation Italians, and Vince and his wife were the only immigrants in the club until very recently when "four or five beautiful people (original immigrants from Italy) of Toronto moved in here and we've become good friends." Two of them are Jim and Virginia Sardo, of Mississauga. Jim, 63, is the former president and CEO of Firestone Canada, and remains an active corporate leader. Jim and Vince hit it off as soon as they met and it's no wonder – Jim's a golfer, a "people person" in the business world, and his own father, Sam, was an immigrant from Italy. "Vince reminds me of my father," said Jim.

"Mr. DTM" — "Down The Middle" DiCosimo and Ida DiCosimo. Vince took up golf when the kids bought him clubs about 15 years ago, and he quickly convinced Ida to get out on the fairways with him. Now she's in a women's league and they both play in and around Niagara Falls and also in Florida. At first Ida thought the ball was "too small," but now she's hitting a good game. They both compete with family members and friends.

Vince admits that he once felt "so alone" as one of the only Italian immigrants in Palm Beach Gardens, that he was even thinking of moving to Fort Lauderdale – but the scene has recently changed. The strictly Italian club holds "Welcome Back" (to Florida) parties each early winter, events for which Vince said even his Jewish friends beg him for an invitation.

Vince used to own and operate a few boats but gave them up. One of them was a 29-footer, which his son, Vince, named "No Vacancy." The children liked boating, and they had fun roaming the intracoastal waterways and the Atlantic Ocean. But Vince admits he was never that big on boating. "I would rather play golf than go on a boat." The corporate executive and business leader admits that he never made a good ship's captain – he never actually felt all that safe on the ocean. "Water makes me nervous," said Vince. "I'm not a water guy. My feet haven't gone in my pool yet."

In Florida, while on vacation, Vince said he just likes to drive around in his two-year-old van, do errands, haunt The Home Depot, putter around the house, tend to his lovely flowers, go for his daily 18-hole golf game (usually around 1 p.m.), read some (he enjoys biographies like those on George Bush, Howard Hughes, Lee Iaccoca.) and socializing with his many friends in the Sunshine State.

"The flowers are unbelievable here. I've got bougainvillea, hibiscus, impatiens…"

He and Ida usually buy their fresh vegetables and fruit at the local market.

Vince gets a kick out of the fact that many people in his wealthy community have not even read the manual on their expensive ovens and always prefer to eat out in the many great local restaurants. Vince and Ida do some of that but Ida cooks, and she especially enjoys cooking when the whole family arrives at Emerald Key Lane. Vince's favourite restaurant is San Gennaro Italian Restaurant in the Crystal

Tree Plaza in North Palm Beach. It's dark, noisy, the food "very tasty" and a guy named Vittorio, from New Jersey, is the host.

Vince is not a newspaper reader, preferring to get his news and entertainment from television, although the weekly shows leave him cold. He admits that he "got stuck and had to learn how to like" such game shows as Wheel of Fortune and Jeopardy, so that he could watch them with his wife. "She likes that Family Feud – I can't stand it. I have no favourite shows now. Before there were better ones, like Happy Days, Hogan's Heroes, Welcome Back Kotter..."

Despite the "spark" of energy and renewal that Ida and Vincent get from their winters in Florida, Vince acknowledges that he is happy to get back to his business responsibilities and to his large family in Niagara Falls. "I am so anxious to go back home at the end," he admits. "Because I have got things to do. I am anxious to get involved again."

Vince said he never considered opening a business in Florida because he believes he's there to relax. "If you get mixed up in some business then it's not a vacation any more; then you have to go back to Niagara Falls to rest."

He said he has been approached by people who want to begin various projects, a donut shop perhaps, or a restaurant, but he's turned them down. "Even my kids have talked about buying a hotel and promote winter packages by being hooked up with a golf course, but, you know what, there are so many down here, you can't even compete. I wouldn't buy a hotel nowhere else but in Niagara Falls. We know the market. We know what's going on. Down here it's not as good as it looks. A lot of people can rent apartments, or condominiums, for a week or months – cheaper than hotel rooms."

Vince and Ida returned from Florida just before Easter this year (2007) and people kidded with them a bit about that. They arrived back in Niagara Falls to spring weather and Vince was anxious to get back out onto the local golf courses.

Then it snowed, and snowed. As late as April 15, the winter coats were coming out again. While back in Palm Beach Gardens, the bougainvilleas were basking in the hot sun.

15

Flying Back to San Lorenzo

"In Italy, they enjoy life more."

V ince is proud of his Italian heritage and happy to go back home from time to time.

"Italy has such a great history. The best artists. Where is another Leonardo Da Vinci, a Michelangelo?

"Even today, being small country with no resources, they do better than any other European country."

Italy also seems to have "some damned smart politicians who play their cards right, I think. They (politicians) are forced to think more because of the limited resources and so many people. Italy is poor, but its government is rich – it takes care of its people."

He and Ida have many Italian friends in Italy, Niagara Falls and Florida. He and his family visit San Lorenzo every year, and stay in touch frequently with relatives and friends in Italy by telephone.

A proud Canadian, who has never regretted that he made his successful life here, Vince said he also tries to impress upon his grandchildren his belief that they should cherish their Italian roots.

About 10 years after Vince and Ida came to Niagara Falls in 1958, they decided that they might move back to Italy and begin a new life with their young children in their homeland. At the time, about 1968, Vince explained, some

Italians in Niagara Falls were doing just that – seeing if they could go back to Italy. The month-long visit was important at the time, said Vince "because our parents didn't even know our kids." By that time, Joe, Frank and Anita were toddlers.

The couple didn't tell anyone in Italy they were thinking of returning for good. They just wanted to "check it out; to look around." They didn't even hint that they were thinking of returning because they didn't want their relatives trying to coax them to make that decision.

But after about a month back in Italy, the couple "reached a mutual agreement to get out of there," and get back to the Falls, said Vince. Ida truly felt that she "could not adjust" again, said her husband.

With Joe, Frank, and Anita they and stayed at the home of Ida's sister, Angelina.

Vince said that after living and working in Canada for 10 years, he was not impressed with the Italian "system." He figured that to make it in business he couldn't do it in his home town area and he would probably have to move to the north, "so felt I may as well stay in Canada."

Ida said she knew she would miss the convenience of modern household appliances. She also didn't see much opportunity there for work and felt the children would eventually have the best opportunities in Canada. "I said it was better to go back home (Niagara Falls), at least I will have something for my kids, a future for my kids."

Vince said the 40-day experiment was good because it settled his mind about ever moving back to Italy and it strengthened his resolve, "my mind was made up," to come back to Niagara Falls "do what I want to do" and become a success.

Vince said some Italian immigrants made the mistake of selling their homes in Niagara Falls and returning to Italy.

"I didn't see anybody who went back from Canada making it big in Italy. I felt I may as well stay in Canada. When I got back, my mind was made up to push for whatever I could do here (in Niagara Falls).

These days, with money to travel, Vince admits that he has "the best of two worlds" because he and family members can return to Italy anytime. They go in May or September and stay for about one month. They usually stay at his wife's sister, Angelina's house and can usually "see everybody" in about one day.

"I cannot live there, but I love to go there and come back," said Vince. "It's funny because it is exciting when you get there but after a week, everything fades away because you see the same people every day. But I do know one thing, in general, in Italy, they enjoy life more. They grew up that way. Now it's changing a little bit. They are getting more Americanized."

When the DiCosimos return to Italy they mostly stay in San Lorenzo and take walks through town.

"It's a very simple life. You get up in the morning. As soon as you go outside the door you can see neighbours, and relatives. Sometimes we go to the bars to have an espresso, but I hate bars. The smoke kills you. I just don't like the crowds. I would rather have a good conversation with somebody on the road."

After about one week, Vince says he begins to relax and slow down. "I've got nothing to think about. After lunch you have got to pick a corner and go to sleep. Have a siesta like the Mexicans. They all wake up around 4 p.m. and go for a walk."

These, days, Vince's sons and daughter have been to San Lorenzo "a lot of times. They love the whole town." All four DiCosimo children can speak Italian.

The Canadian-born Anita, who speaks great Italian,

married Giancarlo Filippelli who is originally from San Lorenzo. Anita met Giancarlo in Connecticut. Vince and Anita were visiting relatives in that state when Anita, 16, met her future husband. Ida and Giancarlo's mother were friends as little girls.

"I saw this tall guy, I didn't pay attention,"Vince recalls. "After we got back, every time I wanted to use the phone, my daughter is on the phone. My wife said 'I think she has found a boyfriend'." (Giancarlo eventually moved to Niagara Falls, N.Y.)

"Giancarlo is such a nice guy," said his father-in-law. "He gets along with my sons like they are brothers."

Vince tries to tell his grandchildren that the DiCosimos have a proud Italian heritage.

"Why do you want to be somebody else?" he asks them. "It's your blood. You got to believe in your roots."

Vince said he never really asked his children if they are proud to be Italian because "I do know that they are."

16

Vince Looks Back on Life

"I am rich because I have my family."

"When I look back, I was a lucky guy because I was never sick," said Vince, reflecting on his life.

"If you've got your health, from there on everything comes together. When I get to this point in my life – and I often tell this to my wife – I have had a beautiful life. I could always do what I wanted to do and if something happens to me now, I won't blink an eye."

Worldly possessions are really "all bullshit," he said. He loves his family above all else for the pride and the joy they have brought to him.

"I am rich because I have my family next to me. That is all."

And, something else that Vince truly believes, and few would dispute this declaration that: "I don't have an enemy in the world." He has had some business disputes with some individuals in Niagara Falls, he admits, but he has tried to be fair and honest with everyone. A few years ago an explosive device destroyed Vince's car while it was parked at their home at 3515 Cardinal Drive. Vince and Ida were in Florida at the time. Vince had left his car outside the garage, as many people do when they are away, to give the appearance of someone being at home. His son, Joe, who lived nearby, heard the explosion. The Niagara Regional Police never laid any charges and the file remains open.

Vince is thankful that over his 71 years he has always been a "free man. I have always done what I had to do because I left my parents at 19, and I didn't have to answer to anybody. That's the freedom that a lot of people have not been able to enjoy. That's a big thing for me."

His two main heroes in life were his parents Anna and Giuseppe whose ideas, morals and beliefs formed his thinking for his first 19 years. He knows the people in his village also looked up to his parents, so he knows they were both excellent role models.

"They provided well for us, and taught us the values in life." When Vince left Italy in 1955, the teachings of his parents and their examples "was all I knew," he pointed out.

Another "hero" is Lee Iaccoca, 83, retired U.S. auto industry executive, best-selling book author, and philanthropist. "That is a guy who I could talk to easily. When I saw him talking, whatever issue it was, he was straightforward. He turned that Chrysler corporation around. They were broke. He had a lot of common sense. When he talked, I could understand him."

Vince likes straightforward people. At meetings he has watched some puffed up people, full of themselves, use 15 words when a few words would do. He also doesn't like to be pushed around by professionals or government types, some of whom, in Vince's view, have "no brains at all."

On his part, he feels he does not take advantage of people but tries to treat everyone with "respect and loyalty." But he stands up to anyone when his own interests are involved – and especially when he knows he just might be right.

He can be a feisty guy. Years ago when he enjoyed the wrestling matches in Niagara Falls, Vince was occasionally so moved at ringside that when one of his favourites was attacked he'd physically take on the other guy. "I was going to kill the son-of-a-bitch. I hit one guy with a chair." The officials warned him not to do it again, but he did. He wasn't ever charged.

These days, "I just let life go by," said Vince. "I never look back. I stick with the decisions I made and make them work. Listen, at the end of the day, nobody is perfect. You learn by mistakes."

In life, Vince does not believe that there is any one set "number or scale," including money, on what you should judge your life. "As long as you are happy. I am rich because I have my family next to me."

His prime advice to his family, including his young grandchildren, is mainly "to be happy. And to try to have some vision about what they want to do in their life.

"Have a goal. But, if for some reason, it doesn't work you have got to be smart enough to say you made a mistake, I have got to jump somewhere else, until you find something that works for you, and you like. Never be scared to work. Do not assume that things are going to work out. But if you believe in something that you want to do, you should never let anything set you back. You have to believe in yourself, first of all.

"I always claim that if I know I am right, I don't back down," he said. This has helped him to move forward on the many business successes he has enjoyed. He knows he got this toughness directly from his mother.

"My mother was the decision maker. She was in control. Dad listened to her. She worked like a slave and she would never take shit from anybody. She had a lot of values, and a good business mind."

Vince said he tells his four children that their children, his grandchildren, "get the best education," and make your own decisions about whether or not to join the DiCosimo family business. It's wise, he said, that any young person, including any of his grandchildren, try out the hotel business during summer vacations from school to see if they are cut out for the challenging hospitality business.

Vince believes that, ultimately, all of his family has the right to decide where they will work. "Be a doctor, be a lawyer, if that's what they want. You've got to make things happen. I always say that things don't just happen, you've gotta make them happen. The easiest thing is to do nothing."

Vince is the eternal optimist. "Tomorrow is going to be a better day. Even if tomorrow is worse than today, you always must believe that the day after is going to be better."

He is not big on lost causes. If something isn't working, his advice is to cut your losses and get out of there.

Vince's other advice to his family is that "good comes from good." (Do some good and it comes back to you.)

He said that he generally "trusts everybody," but that trust must be earned. "I can also be suspicious of everybody."

His son, Vince Jr., said his dad is a "simple guy" and by that he means that his father is not a braggart, loves the simple ways and joys of life, and is also old fashioned in many ways. For example, his grandchildren bought Vince a $1,500 laptop computer, but Vince isn't too eager to learn to use it. He does not own a BlackBerry, although he loves his cell phones. His ring is the lively *William Tell* Overture by Gioacchino Rossini. To write up the day's "to do" list, and to record the names and phone numbers of his hundreds of business contacts, Vince uses cheap, plain white paper placemats that he buys from a discount store. When he fills one mat, he folds it up, stores it, and starts another sheet. He has his own filing system for his place mats – they are stacked according to date, and he says he has no trouble retrieving a name or number.

Vince admits to some mistakes through the years but he believes that he was smart enough to realize that they were mistakes, so be made the needed changes right away, without delay. "But, I will tell you, a few mistakes made in the many, many business ventures I have been involved with is not that bad," Vince said.

His said he learned the lesson from his mother that one should not be envious of other people. "Never, never wish that they will do badly my mother used to say. That is bad for you. And that's my philosophy. In Niagara Falls I always hang around with guys who are better off than me. I am just happy that they accept me as their friend. I look up to them in a sense. I never put myself down, either."

His advice to his grandchildren is to not be envious of other people, nor want what they have. "You have to set your focus for yourself, you can't be looking at the other guy and thinking how you can be like that guy. Don't worry about him; worry about yourself. Set your goal and go for it. And you have gotta have the will to work. Never count the hours you work, and also you gotta have a little bit of guts."

Despite having attained only Grade 5 education, Vince said he is not intimidated by anyone with a higher formal education. And he's "comfortable" with anyone in business either at the boardroom table or the dinner table.

He enjoys meeting people from all walks of life "one on one."

"I think I can keep up with anybody (in conversation) about anything. I can talk to a teacher, a lawyer, a doctor. I never get stuck. They can't say I am dumb. That's the way I am. I like to know things." He has also found that it is often the case that the higher the education an individual has, "the less you can understand him or her." He added that some highly educated folks take 15 words to say something that can be said in three words.

Vince would certainly subscribe to these wise words of General Dwight D. Eisenhower, who became a U.S. president:

"An intellectual is a man who takes more words than necessary to tell more than he knows." Vince, who reads widely and is curious about many subjects, said he feels sorry for any person who is comfortable only when talking about his or her own business or any other narrow line of work. "Some of these guys embarrass me in front of other people."

He feels that when they are talking on a wide range of subjects "I can keep up with them," because he reads quite a bit, mostly in English, but occasionally in Italian.

Vince's congenial way with people results in his adult children, who are his business partners, asking their father to meet new clients to break the ice and get things going. "So, I meet with them and I connect right away. I set things up. And then I leave them with the kids and we become friends."

"My kids work harder than me; they are very dedicated," said the proud father. He pointed out that his children are independent thinkers, but once a common decision is made they move forward together. Each child has a position and a responsibility in the company and they all work well together.

Ida DiCosimo agrees completely. She said the family business team is a true "democracy." But they respect the opinions of their father. "They (children) know what to do – but they need their father. They want his support."

In Vince's view, hard work and saving money has been the way of life of many Italian immigrants, himself included. He always believed that he would become well off. He became ambitious early in life, could never envision limits to what could be done. He also knows he was "fearless."

Even as a young boy, Vince repeatedly told his parents that he couldn't stay on the farm because that work was simply not for him. "Work never bothered me. I could work 24 hours a day. I never got tired." He was not afraid of hard work, but it had to be "different work" than farming – and it had to pay.

"I said that I had to find a way to become rich. I always had a dream to become wealthy but that didn't have to be in hotels. Anything. I wanted to be well off."

In his own way, he believes that he's always been a "visionary" who came up with ideas and did his best to follow through on them.

If anyone asks Vince his secret of success, he answers that he was never scared of failure, never afraid of a challenge, never afraid of risking money. Business was "a game I had to win. Whatever it took to do it."

In the early years of business and family raising, "I didn't have a holiday for 24 years. I never complained."

Vince has seen people go bankrupt and he doesn't believe you can blame the economy. There are just too many factors involved in business failures. Too many people go into business thinking they'll get rich quick, he cautions.

"All of a sudden they run into tough times. Those are the times that the individual has to stay around, fight it out. The majority of people, I think, are very weak. They are not fighters. They just give it up. Sometimes you have to be very creative to survive."

Vince said he was never afraid to take personal responsibility for all loans he incurred no matter what size or what interest rate charged because he always believed in himself and in his plans.

Vince believes he had always honoured his commitments. "I do know that from the first day that I had a mortgage on my house I never, never missed a payment. There were times that I didn't have a penny on my pocket. There were times when, if my wife needed a light bulb, that I couldn't buy it. I didn't care. I took care of my obligations first. It is very important that you do that."

Years ago, one of his suppliers told Vince he was scared because the tourism industry was slumping and Vince responded to him that "the easiest thing in the world is to be scared. When things are bad, everybody is in the same boat."

Vince notes that "banks need people like me to make money, but we need the banks. If things are bad, I tell the banks that I am the same guy as I was when I signed. I am still the same good guy. If things are going wrong (in the economy) it's not my fault. We live together."

Vince was an idea man even as a kid. He says that it bothered him in his home village that "people from out of town" would collect the local milk in a truck and take it away.

"So I told my father that we've gotta open a dairy." His father replied to his son that when he grew up "you can have a dairy factory in your own house, I don't like it in my house."

Years later, in about 1959, even while he was working as a labourer in Niagara Falls, the enterprising spirit was strong in the recent immigrant. In an attempt to make extra money, he and his wife once picked cherries in Niagara-on-the-Lake, loaded them up, along with strawberries, in a pickup. Then Vince was off to market in Toronto to begin making his fortune.

He'd never been to Toronto. He didn't even know where the market was. But he was stopped by an inspector on the highway who claimed his strawberries were going bad. He went home. He handed over the fruit to a local kid who sold the produce door to door and Vince recovered his costs. His first business venture had "failed pretty bad."

These days Vince and his family employ hundreds of people.

"Personally I always felt that I could handle people to work for me," he says. "Let the people do the work, and make sure I manage right."

Vince is proud to say that, even today, when they meet him on the street, employees from 40 or so years ago "say thank you very much.

"At first, when I started to have people, I was the kinda guy who would show them what to do. Make sure they understand what I want them to do. Let them do it and keep an eye on them.

"My philosophy, and I tell my kids too, and I believe this too – I trust people. I trust everybody, but I am suspicious of anybody. What it means is that I keep an eye on everybody. If you want to be trusted, show me you can be trusted. It doesn't matter if it is a chef or the sweeper, if you treat them with respect, tell them the truth, and show them you are not a fake. If you like them you have to show them that you like them, not because they work for you, but you have to like them as a person.

"If they do something wrong you have to tell them. But they have to have the freedom to do the job. If you are always behind their back they will feel nervous that they can never do the job right."

Vince detests business people who are "all words" and no action, those who are "preachy," and "put on a front," but have no substance. Those people who "make up what they have never done in life by talking."

When he and his wife are in Florida, his kids are in charge of business . But he does call back to Niagara Falls every morning to check on a few figures, such as room occupancy.

Vince tries to tell his managers (such as his maintenance engineers, for example) that some of them "start working before they start thinking. I tell them that they have got to look, think, move away, make your brains work – even go back the next day. Make sure in your mind that you can see everything working and then it is so easy to do it."

Vince prides himself on the fact that he built, with his own hands, much of the equipment for his early businesses, such as the automated car wash and the tables and chairs for his first eatery on River Road. For this reason, he has a practical outlook on things. He's a "hands-on" guy even today, offering his employees advice in the day-to-day operations.

"I built my own (car wash) conveyer, brushes, everything. I wasn't afraid to get dirty. I always find the easiest, fastest and cheapest way."

Vince admits that, besides the nuts and bolts problems in his commercial empires, his biggest management enjoyment is "definitely" his employees and his customers.

"I love people. I like to talk to people. I like to help people." Help, yes, and he gives well to charity but, in the tough world of business, Vincent has learned that you can't be "Santa Claus." He expects his people to produce to be paid.

He'll occasionally chat up his guests on the hotel elevator, or elsewhere, to "make sure that my people have treated them right."

Vince knows that in the hospitality business you cannot satisfy people "one hundred percent. So, what you do you try to the best to make sure that everything is done right."

Vince knows that whatever rate he charges, the customer must receive his money's worth. He believes it should only be necessary to thank any customer "just once" for coming to his hotel. After that, if he and his employees are doing things right, the customer will be thanking his staff again and again for making their stay enjoyable.

"Treat people with respect. Like royalty.

"That's all you need."

17

A Look Into the Future

"If I build my own golf course, I can play when I want to."

R etire?

"Never," said Vince DiCosimo.

The 71-year-old said his health is good, his beloved family works along with him, and he has some more big plans.

"One thing about me," Vince confides. "I never give up the dream, the idea."

"When I got to 45 years old, I said 'What a stupid guy I have been, why do I set myself a date to retire, why don't I keep working and whatever happens, happens'? All my dreams, to be honest with you, they became better than I thought!"

"Me and my wife built the engine of success but my family is driving the engine. They are so good at it. My accomplishments in life have nothing to do with money because we have got no money."

His children, his business partners, are all "workaholics." Never has he heard one of his children complain, "even as a joke," that they are overworked.

Vince still has dreams. He knows they will come true.

Following completion of the 58-storey wing to the Hilton Niagara Falls Fallsview, there are some other DiCosimo projects being planned. One is a major golf course, restaurant, vineyard and winery.

"If I build my own golf course, I can play when I want to," said Vince with a laugh.

The DiCosimo family has purchased about 300 acres of land off Mountain Road near the edge of the escarpment in Niagara Falls. On that property, the course would be laid out with the assistance of a top "name" course designer. Near the course would be vineyards and a winery.

The whole project could cost from $15 to $20 million, Vince revealed. Access to the course would be tied closely to the guest list at the Niagara Hilton Fallsview. The DiCosimo winery would also be tied in closely to the hotel that is now a popular convention accommodation. Vince said convention guests typically stay two or three days, so free games of golf and visits to a first class Niagara winery and restaurant, would be natural tie-ins with the visits.

"The main thing is that we have got the land. Even if I have got to get partners, I don't mind."

Vince said he is negotiating with Piero Antinori, the president of "Antinori," one of the largest wine producers in Italy. He hopes Mr. Antinori's famous company, founded in 1385, can enter into a partnership with the DiCosimo winery. Vince threw a party for Piero Antinori at The Hilton "and we connected right away."

"He is a very smart man, very polite, very classy. I talked with him about what I wanted to do and he liked it. He said 'Vincenzo, I am interested'."

Vince said that he also has had some telephone talks with Piero and met with him at a private Toronto club. He said the Italian gentleman, who is heralded as "The Prince of Italian Vintners," is particularly interested in the production of Canadian ice wines. He said he wants Vince to contact him when the DiCosimos are ready to build their winery.

"I would love to call it 'Antinori of Niagara'."

His son, Joe, is now heading up the planning for the golf course/winery venture. Joe, a golfer like his father, hopes to have a hand in the course design. Vince would like to start building out on Mountain Road in about 2009.

In the future, Vince would like his children to make the major decisions concerning the family's various businesses. He said he respects their judgment, knows that they are all the "best of friends" with each other and get along well with each other. His children are a team, he said, and they decide by consensus.

"I am a lucky man."

Photo: David Haskell

The DiCosimo family in the lobby of the Hilton Niagara Falls Fallsview in 2006. From the left are Joe, Anita, Vince, Ida, Frank, and Vince Jr

18

The Woman Behind the Man

"Everything is good now."

The old saying that "behind every successful man is a woman" has never been truer than in the case of Ida DiCosimo.

Vince and the couple's children credit Ida with being the unselfish, hardworking, and understanding marriage partner and mother who held the family together with love and strength. She was there, and is there, for Vince, the children, and grandchildren through good and bad times.

Vince says Ida has been the key to his happiness and to his success.

Ida said she and Vince have never had a serious fight. Disagreements, yes. In tribute to her kind and "gentle" man, Ida said that through all of their struggles, all of the hardships, Vince never, ever, laid a hand on her or on the children. "I have never seen my husband really mad. Never!" Vince is never even in a bad mood, said his wife. She believes that Vince got his gentle ways from his father. Even when Joe and Frank as kids would get into a fight, and they did that often growing up, gentle Vince usually handled it by simply saying: "Leave it alone; don't worry about it."

"Vince and me? We had no need to fight," she explains. In their early years of marriage they couldn't fight over money, the source of most marriage problems, because there simply was no money to fight about. She adds that another source of calm in the early Niagara Falls years was that neither her parents nor Vince's were here to perhaps complicate matters. They were on their own.

What money they had through the years went toward raising the children and paying the mortgage. "I never bought anything for me, first it was for the kids. I always saved a thousand dollars not spend a thousand dollars." Ida said neither she nor Vince ever wanted very much and they were always frugal.

But Ida pointed out, with a laugh, Vince would sometimes buy "stupid things," and she was always there to point that out. He has a strange fascination for products advertised on television and he wants to buy a lot of the things he sees. "Those things on TV always look good," she said. "Those knives cut, boom boom, but when you bring them home they are a piece of junk."

She also noted that Vince loves The Home Depot, buys like mad there, and ends up taking a lot of things back. (She thinks there are possibly 10 coffee makers in the DiCosimo garage.)

Ida admits that raising the four children without their grandparents here, nor very much other family support, was quite tough at times. Also, she worked outside the DiCosimo home, and at various businesses, at Niagara Rug, to bring in more money. For instance, when Ida finished her eight hours at Niagara Rug, she'd head over to Jumbo Burger Villa. For the first three years of their marriage Vince wanted to get established so kids were out of the picture,"but I wanted kids."

Ida admits she is a worrier and always has been. She's worried now that the Hilton is getting too big and that her husband and boys will get hurt on the construction site.

Years ago she'd cry when Vince would come home and announce that they were in debt again over some property purchase. But she'd calm down when she realized that Vince probably made a good deal. She is worried today about the $200-million, 58-storey addition the family is having built on their Hilton Niagara Falls Fallsview. "It's too big," she said with a laugh.

Ida added that she was broken hearted when all of the family's many Niagara Falls businesses were sold in the last few years to finance the new project. She explained that many years of family work went into their properties.

"I cried, those things have lots of memories for me. For one year now I have never gone back to River Road."

Asked what drove Vince to success, Ida explained that he must have got his strong ambition from his mother, Anna. "Not his father." From an early age, she knows that Vince wanted to make his mark in business. He didn't come to Canada to dig ditches "or he would have gone home to work on the farm." She noted that Vince worked many nights while he ran the steel business because he would be with engineers and architects in the off hours studying building plans so that he could learn to estimate the costs of various jobs and how to bid on them.

It has been important to Ida, she said, to live to see all of her grandchildren confirmed in the church and hopefully some day be at their weddings. "Seeing all my children and grandchildren baptized, first communion, what else do I want?

"I want time for myself," she said, but she also wants to "know everything" about what's going on in the family. Vince doesn't always tell her exactly what is going on in the DiCosimo business; he will usually just tell his wife that "everything is fine." It is at that exact time that Ida will "pick up the phone and call Joey. Joey will tell me."

Ida delights in her husband's eternal optimism. Even in the early 1990s, when things got tight in the DiCosimo businesses, Vince always told her that if everything failed, "don't worry, we'll start again."

She said her husband must remain active in his businesses. He likes to be near the action at the hotel. Even when he and Ida take a month off to visit relatives in San Lorenzo, Vince gets restless to get back to Canada, she said. Also, Ida said with a laugh, Vince wants to golf all the time and the closest good place to play when they are in Italy is in Milano.

Ida believes that she and Vince, because they worked hard all their lives, deserve some time for themselves now and also a lightened work load.

"Everything is good now."

Ida said she's got "good kids" who have good spouses. She is happy that all of her children feel it's important to leave work at the proper time and go home for dinner with their families each evening.

"And, on Sunday they spend time at home."

Ida knows that when the 58-storey addition to their Hilton hotel is opened in 2009 it will be a grand occasion for the family.

She and Vince will have been married for more than half a century. They will be standing there at the ribbon cutting with their children and grandchildren and with their loyal employees and other many friends.

"Mr. D." will say only a few words, as always, but he will not have to say much. The love and respect of the people surrounding him will say everything about Vincenzo DiCosimo.

"Mr. D." Una bella vita

Photo: Kevin Argue

Vince DiCosimo with Dalton McGuinty, Premier of Ontario, Niagara-on-the-Lake,
August 13, 2007.